Landscapes of TENERIFE

a countryside guide

Third edition

Noel Rochford

SUNFLOWER BOOKS

For Ramona

Third edition

Sunflower Books
12 Kendrick Mews
London SW7 3HG, UK

First published 1984
Second edition 1989

ISBN 1-85691-047-4

Dragon tree (Dracaena draco)

Important note to the reader

We have tried to ensure that the descriptions and maps in this book are error-free at press date. The book will be updated, where necessary, whenever future printings permit. It will be very helpful for us to receive your comments (sent in care of the publishers, please) for the updating of future printings.

We also rely on those who use this book — especially walkers — to take along a good supply of common sense when they explore. Conditions change fairly rapidly on Tenerife , and ***storm damage or bulldozing may make a route unsafe at any time***. If the route is not as we outline it here, and your way ahead is not secure, return to the point of departure. ***Never attempt to complete a tour or walk under hazardous conditions!*** Please read carefully the notes on pages 31 to 38, as well as the introductory comments at the beginning of each tour and walk (regarding road conditions, equipment, grade, distances and time, etc). Explore ***safely***, while at the same time respecting the beauty of the countryside.

Cover photograph: the Barranco del Tomadero (Walk 19), below the the twin peaks of Los Hermanos (photograph: Andreas Stieglitz)
Title page: one of the statues of Guanche chiefs at La Candelaria (Car tour 5)
Photographs by the author, except for those on pages 17, 18, 21, 23, 25, 26, 28, 30-31, 50, 51, 59, 66-67, 79, 92, 100, 104, 110, (Andreas Stieglitz) and 63, 68-69, 72 (John Underwood)
Maps by John Theasby and Pat Underwood
Drawings by Sharon Rochford
A CIP catalogue record for this book is available from the British Library.
Printed and bound in the UK by Brightsea Press, Exeter

10 9 8 7 6 5 4 3 2 1

Contents

Preface

Tenerife has something for everyone — country lanes for strolling, nature trails for hiking, mountains to be scaled, and beaches where you can offer up your tired limbs to the warmth of her sun.

To absorb and appreciate Tenerife's beauty takes time. Her personality lies in the countryside, and her moods are captured at sunrise and sunset. The bleak south is a mystery of dry terraced slopes, sliced through by deep ravines. The lush and green northern escarpment yields up forested hillsides rolling off the central massif, soon burgeoning with produce as it steps its way down to an indigo sea. Las Cañadas, the focal point of every visit, lies embedded in the island's backbone. Pine-studded slopes lead you up to this world apart, where strange hues and tormented rock forms are dominated by the majesty of El Teide.

Tenerife's costumes, embroidered with seasonal flora, are constantly changed for your pleasure. In spring the island is a living tapestry of colour. This is the best time for exploring. The profusion of wild plants and flowers makes the island a botanical treasure. But remember, no season is without its bloom and pot-pourri of colour.

You needn't be a walker to appreciate Tenerife's beauty. The car tours, with their encompassing panoramas, will give you a taste of the landscapes. The picnic spots will, I hope, encourage you to meander just a little further on. Then there are several short walks that require no great expenditure of energy and make a memorable day's excursion. Getting off the main roads is discovering Tenerife.

Walkers, your affair with Tenerife is about to begin. She has so much with which to entice you — sculpted crags, deep and shaded ravines, fern-drenched laurel forests, majestic pines and tapestries of terracing falling away to the sea.

The Canary islanders' warmth and friendliness are best preserved in the countryside. Here they still have time. A friendly smile breaks down

Margarita del Teide (Argytanthemum anethifolium)

Cardón (Euphorbia canariensis)

all communication barriers and, before you know it, you will be on your way with an armful of fruit. These will be your most treasured memories.

My love for Tenerife led me into the depths of the countryside years ago. My short strolls soon turned into longer rambles and these, in turn, became long hikes. I'd become an avid walker and explorer. The fact that I saw so few other walkers prompted me to write the book — to encourage you to step off the usual touring routes, to see and feel the real Tenerife. There's an unending source of weird and wonderful landscapes just awaiting your exploration, and I hope that *Landscapes of Tenerife* will help you find them.

Acknowledgements

I would like to express my gratitude to the following people, for their invaluable help:

Isidoro Sánchez García of ICONA, for information and maps; F Opelio Rodriguez Peña of the Delegación del Ministerio de Comercio y Turismo, for information and brochures; the local government offices (Cabildo) and the Department of Public Works in Santa Cruz, for maps; the Servicio Geográfico del Ejercito in Madrid, for permission to adapt their large scale maps.

The Grupo Montañero de Tenerife for information, guiding, and their constant encouragement (especially Edmundo Herrero Rello and Rafael Valencia).

Luís Rodriguez Rivero for his help and information.

My publisher, Pat Underwood, for her support.

My sister, Sharon, for her splendid drawings.

My parents and friends, who were all so supportive throughout.

Finally, very special thanks to two wonderful people to whom I am very much indebted: Edmundo Herrero Rello, of Tenerife's mountaineering club, for all those hours he devoted to teaching me the secrets of Tenerife, and Ramona, for all her typing, proof-reading, correcting, walk-checking and simply keeping me on an even keel!

Useful books

Bramwell, D, and Bramwell, Z *Wild Flowers of the Canary Islands,* London, Stanley Thornes

Cano, D M *Tenerife,* León, Editorial Everest (available on the island)

Cuscoy, L D and Larsen, P C *The Book of Tenerife,* Santa Cruz de Tenerife, Instituto de Estudios Canarios (available on the island)

Moeller, H *The Flora of the Canary Islands,* Puerto de la Cruz, Fred Kolbe (available on the island)

Also available: Rochford, Noel *Landscapes of Gran Canaria, Landscapes of Southern Tenerife and La Gomera, Landscapes of La Palma and El Hierro, Landscapes of Fuerteventura, Landscapes of Lanzarote* (Sunflower Books)

 Getting about

There is no doubt that a **hired car** is the most convenient way of getting about Tenerife, and car rental on the island is good value, especially if you shop around.

The second most flexible form of transport is a hired **taxi** and, especially if three or four people are sharing the cost, this becomes an attractive idea. If you're making an unmetered journey, do agree on the price *before* setting out: all taxi drivers should carry an official price list.

Coach tours are the most popular way of seeing many holiday islands; this is an easy way to get to know a place in comfort, before embarking on your own adventures.

My favourite way of getting about is by **local bus.** The system is very economical, reliable, and fun! You get splendid views perched up on bus seats, as they bump their way around the island. The plans on the following two pages show you where to board buses in Puerto and Santa Cruz. On pages 128-132 you will find timetables for all the buses used for the walks and picnics in this book. But please do not rely *solely* on the timetables included here: changes are fairly frequent. When you arrive on the island, obtain the latest bus timetables from your local bus station or, if you go to Santa Cruz, get timetables at the station there (they are the most ample and up-to-date). It always pays to verify bus departures and returns for the longer journeys *before* setting out, and it always pays to arrive a bit *early!* Most of the buses used are operated by one company, TITSA. (You can purchase a fare-saver 'TITSA-Bono' bus card in advance.) A few buses, to the Anaga Peninsula, are operated by TRANSMERSA out of a modern bus station near the motorway at La Laguna. The station is shared with TITSA, and all TITSA buses from Puerto or Santa Cruz stop there, so it is easy to change buses.

Taginaste rojo (Eichium wildpretti)

PUERTO DE LA CRUZ

1 Tourist information
2 Town hall (Ayuntamiento)
3 Casa Iriarte
4 Post office
5 Nuestra Señora de la Peña
6 Castillo de San Felipe
7 Municipal maritime park (to be built)
8 Casino Taoro
9 Bull ring
10 Bus station
11 to Botanical gardens
12 Puerto Pesquero

city exits

Exit A (the Carretera del Norte) leads to the C820 and La Orotava

Exit B (Avenida de Colón) leads to the motorway to La Laguna and Santa Cruz

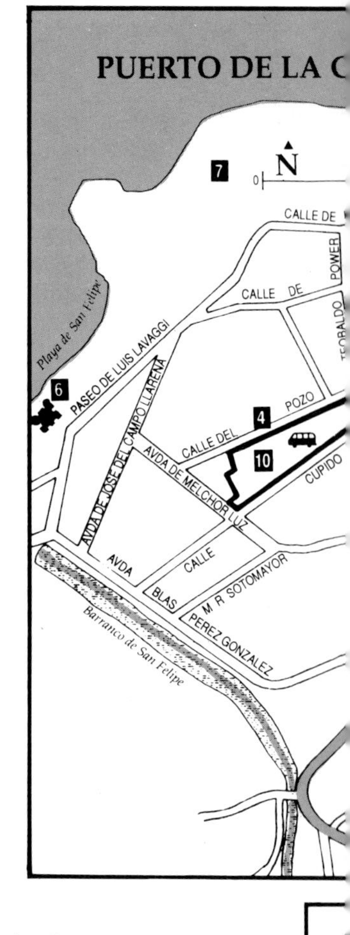

SANTA CRUZ

1 Plaza de España
2 Cabildo (local government headquarters), Tourist information, Archaeological museum
3 San Francisco church, Municipal museum of fine arts
4 Post office
5 Plaza de Weyler
6 Market
7 Bus station
8 Plaza del Príncipe
9 Plaza de la Candelaria

city exits

Exit A (Avenida 3 de Mayo) leads to the motorways north and south

Exit B (Avenida Anaga) leads to San Andrés and the northern Anaga via El Bailadero

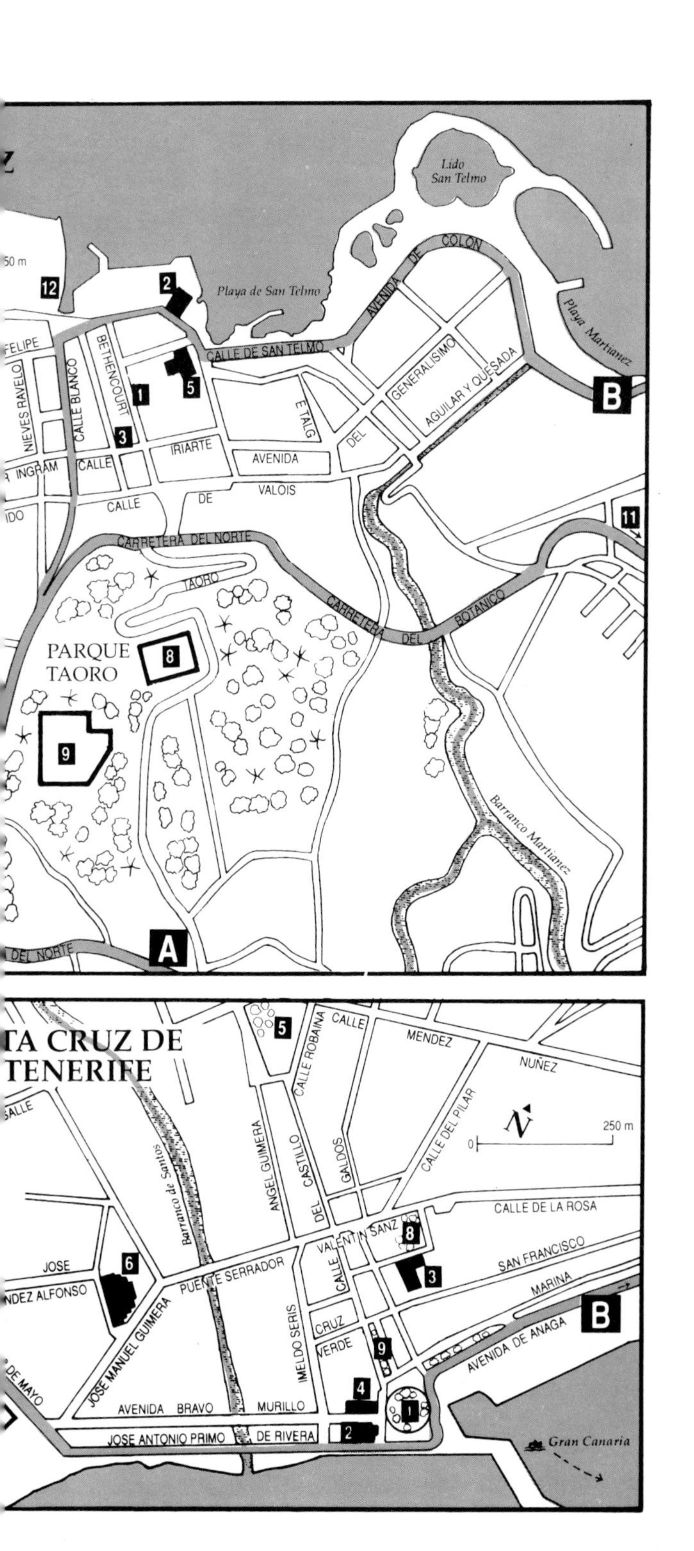

Lido San Telmo
Playa de San Telmo
AVENIDA DE COLON
Playa Martianez
CALLE DE SAN TELMO
GENERALISIMO
AGUILAR Y QUESADA
DEL
AVENIDA
IRIARTE
CALLE BLANCO
BETHENCOURT
NIEVES RAVELO
FELIPE
INGRAM
CALLE
CALLE DE VALOIS
CARRETERA DEL NORTE
TAORO
CARRETERA DEL BOTANICO
PARQUE TAORO
Barranco Martianez
DEL NORTE
A
B
TA CRUZ DE TENERIFE
CALLE MENDEZ NUÑEZ
CALLE ROBAINA
CALLE DEL PILAR
ANGEL GUIMERA
DEL CASTILLO
GALDOS
N
0
250 m
CALLE DE LA ROSA
VALENTIN SANZ
SAN FRANCISCO
MARINA
AVENIDA DE ANAGA
Barranco de Santos
PUENTE SERRADOR
JOSE
NDEZ ALFONSO
JOSE MANUEL GUIMERA
IMELDO SERIS
CALLE
CRUZ VERDE
DE MAYO
AVENIDA BRAVO MURILLO
JOSE ANTONIO PRIMO DE RIVERA
Gran Canaria

Picnicking

Picnickers are extremely well catered for on Tenerife. ICONA (Spain's national nature conservation agency) and the island government have worked together to set up several very well-equipped 'recreation areas' around the island. At these *zonas recreativas* (which tend to be crowded on weekends and holidays), you'll find tables and benches, barbecues, WCs, drinking fountains and play areas for children. They've also scattered simple little wooden shelters, with tables and benches, in some of the island's loveliest settings. You'll find many of these *chozas* along the C821 (the 'Las Cañadas road') and in the Orotava valley.

All **roadside** picnic areas **with tables** (and sometimes other facilities) are indicated both in the car touring notes and on the touring and walking maps by the symbol ⛩. They are also briefly described on the following pages, together with suggestions for picnics 'off the beaten track'.

All the information you need to get to any of the picnics suggested is given on the following pages. *Picnic numbers correspond to walk numbers,* so you can quickly find the general location on the island by looking at the colour map, where the walks are outlined in white. I give transport details (🚌: bus numbers; 🚗: where to park), walking times, and views or setting. Beside the picnic title, you'll find a map reference: the exact location of the picnic spot is shown on this *walking map* by the symbol ***P***.

Please glance over the comments *before* you set off: if some walking is involved, remember to wear sensible shoes and to **take a sunhat** (○ indicates a picnic in **full sun**). It's a good idea to take along a plastic groundsheet as well, in case the ground is damp or prickly.

If you are travelling to your picnic by bus, be sure to arm yourself with up-to-date bus timetables (see page 7). **If you are travelling to your picnic by car**, be extra vigilant off the main roads: children and animals are often in the village streets. Without damaging plants, do park *well off* the road; **never** block a road or track. **All picnickers should read the country code on page 37 and go quietly in the countryside.**

2 CHOZA CHIMOCHE (map pages 52-53, drawing page 41)

by car or taxi: 45min on foot *by bus: 45min on foot*

🚗 either at the Bermeja picnic area or at the Choza Chimoche turn-off, at the beginning of the track (both are on the C821, about 4km south of Aguamansa; see map pages 52-53). Car tour 1

🚌 348: ask to be put off at 'Choza Bermeja'.

Walk east on the forestry track just south of the Bermeja *choza.* You'll come to Choza Chimoche after a gentle climb of about 45 minutes. A few minutes past here is another picnic spot, at the mouth of a dry *barranco* (the Barranco de Pedro Gil). Shade. The bottom photograph on page 60 shows a nearby setting.

4 CHOZA EL TOPO (map pages 52-53)

by car or taxi: 1h on foot *by bus: 1h on foot*

🚗 La Caldera car park (C821). Car tour 1

🚌 345 to La Caldera

Follow Short walk 4 (page 44). There's no climbing. Views over Aguamansa's valley. Shade. En route you pass through the settings shown on pages 58 and 60.

5a LA CALDERA (map pages 52-53)

by car or taxi: up to 5min on foot *by bus: up to 5min on foot*

🚗 La Caldera car park (C821). Car tour 1

🚌 345 to La Caldera

Zona recreativa with full facilities (see page 10). Views over the Orotava Valley similar to those on page 21.

5b CHOZA PEREZ VENTOSO (map pages 52-53)

by car or taxi: 30min on foot *by bus: 30min on foot*

🚗 trout farm car park or the bar/restaurant just north of the trout farm (C821, just south of Aguamansa). Car tour 1

🚌 345 to Aguamansa

Follow the C821 downhill: 100m/yds below the bar/ restaurant pass the bus shelter. Head downhill to Aguamansa from the bus shelter (signposted). A few minutes down, take the first right turn (for 'Mamio, Pinoleris, and La Florida'). Follow this tarred lane (photograph at the bottom of page 51) for about 15 minutes, then keep left at a junction. Pass a shrine a few minutes later, then turn right on a farm track to the *choza.* No climbing. Shade.

6 LA CRUCITA (map pages 52-53/56-57, photograph pages 54-55) ○

by car or taxi: 5-30min on foot *by bus: not easily accessible*

🚗 on the forestry track at La Crucita, 13km east of El Portillo on the C824 (signposted). Car tour 5

Picnic by the side of the track, or explore either side of

the C824. If you go west, you'll have views of the Orotava Valley and El Teide; to the east you would overlook Montaña de las Arenas (photograph pages 54-55). *Note that these descents are steep and slippery, and that there is no shade.*

7a CHOZA MONTAÑA ALTA (map pages 60-61)

by car or taxi: up to 5min on foot — *by bus: 15-20min on foot*

at Montaña Alta. Car tours 1, 5 — 348 to El Portillo

From El Portillo head east on the C824: the *choza* can be seen on the north side of the road after 1km. Views of El Teide. Shade at the shelter.

7b-g LAS CAÑADAS ROAD (touring map)

There are six ICONA *chozas* on the C821 (the 'Las Cañadas road'; Car tour 1) between Aguamansa and El Portillo; all are signposted with the letter 'P'. Shade.

- 7b Choza Bermeja: north side of the road; shelter, tables, benches
- 7c Choza Margarita de Piedra: north side of the road, near the famous stone 'daisy' shown here; shelter
- 7d Choza Wildpret: south side of the road; shelter, tables, benches
- 7e Choza Leoncio Rodriguez: north side of the road; shelter
- 7f Choza Bethencourt: north side of the road; shelter
- 7g Choza Sventenius: north side of the road; shelter

Margarita de Piedra

10 LOS ROQUES DE GARCIA (map pages 70-71, photographs pages 68-69, 72) ○

by car or taxi: 5-20min on foot — *by bus: 5-20min on foot*

at the Los Roques car park (on the west side of the C821, near the Parador). Car tour 1

348 to the Parador de las Cañadas

Follow Walk 10 for a short time, or just amble about until you find a comfortable rock. Marvellous views of El Teide, Guajara and the weird rock formations, but the only shade is from the rocks themselves.

11 PIEDRAS AMARILLAS (map pages 70-71, photographs page 17, 63, 72) ○

by car or taxi: 15-20min on foot — *by bus: 15-20min on foot*

at the Parador. Car tour 1 — 348 to the Parador

Follow Walk 11 (page 72) to the 'Yellow Stones'. No shade.

12a CHANAJIGA (map page 77) ⛩

by car or taxi: up to 5min on foot *by bus: not easily accessible*
Chanajiga car park: heading south from La Orotava on the C821, turn right on the TF2125 (towards Benijos and Palo Blanco). The turn-off for Chanajiga is at Las Llanadas (signposted). Near Car tour 1
Zona recreativa with full facilities (see page 10).

12b CAÑADA DE LOS GUANCHEROS (map page 77, photographs pages 59, 75) ○

by car or taxi: 15-55min on foot *by bus: 15-55min on foot*
Las Cañadas Visitors' Centre (C821 near El Portillo). Car tours 1, 5
348 to El Portillo
Follow Walk 12 (page 74) to picnic in the setting shown on page 75 (15min) or walk on to the *cañada* (55min), from where you will have the view shown on page 59. No shade.

13 LA CORONA (map page 80, photograph page 79)

by car or taxi: up to 5min on foot *by bus: 1h on foot*
at the La Corona *mirador*/restaurant: from Icod el Alto, continue west on the TF221 towards La Guancha. Take the first tarred turn-off left, about five minutes west of Icod. Near Car tour 3
354 to Icod el Alto; then follow Walk 13 (page 78) — a very steep climb of 250m/800ft.
Overlooks the entire Orotava Valley to the eastern escarpment. Trees.

14 EL LAGAR (map pages 82-83) ⛩

by car or taxi: up to 5min on foot *by bus: not easily accessible*
at El Lagar: head west for La Guancha on the TF221. In the town, take the first turning left, just past the petrol station. From here on, the way to El Lagar is signposted. If approaching La Guancha from the west, take a right turn just *before* the petrol station. Car tour 3
Large *zona recreativa* (see page 10) in the shade of pines. Nearby settings are shown on pages 84 and 89.

16 LAS ARENAS NEGRAS (map pages 90-91, photograph page 92) ⛩

by car or taxi: 1h on foot *by bus: 1h on foot*
car park at La Montañeta. The TF2225 climbs the slopes above Icod de los Vinos, and the road to La Montañeta lies to the south of Icod, halfway round this road. There's a forestry house just above La Montañeta. The local people drive up the rough track all the way to the picnic grounds, but this is not recommended with a hired car, since you are not likely to be insured for damage to tyres. Car tour 3
363 to Icod de los Vinos and 360 from Icod to La Montañeta
Follow Walk 16 (page 90) to Las Arenas Negras, a steep climb of 250m/800ft. Shade of pines and full *zona recreativa* facilities (see page 10). Busy on weekends: to get away from the crowd, continue uphill past the picnic grounds for another 10-20 minutes.

17 NEAR ERJOS (map pages 94-95) ○

by car or taxi: 10-55min on foot *by bus: 10-55min on foot*
🚗 at Erjos (C820, between El Tanque and Santiago). Car tour 3
🚌 363 to Icod de los Vinos and 🚌 460 to Erjos

Follow Walk 17 (page 93) as far as you like. Soon there are views to El Teide, and you can picnic beside the track. Gentle climb back to your transport.

18 PUNTA DEL FRAILE (map page 98-99) ○

by car or taxi: up to 5min on foot *by bus: 45-50min on foot*
🚗 at Punta del Fraile. Car tour 3
🚌 363 to Icod de los Vinos and 🚌 366 to Buenavista

By car or on foot, follow the TF1429 from Buenavista towards the Teno lighthouse, until you come to the Punta del Fraile *mirador* on your right after 3km. No shade, but the coastal outlook over Buenavista and the jagged cliffs is spectacular.

19a PLAYA DE LOS TROCHES (map on reverse of touring map) ○

by car or taxi: 10-15min on foot *by bus: 10-15min on foot*
🚗 roundabout at the end of the TF121, beyond Punta del Hidalgo. Car tour 4
🚌 105 to Punta del Hidalgo

Follow Walk 19 (page 100) to this stony beach. Steep descent and ascent. The only shade is from the cliffs.

19b LAS ESCALERAS (map on reverse of touring map)

by car or taxi: 35min on foot *by bus: 35min on foot*
🚗 Las Carboneras: the road is 1km east of Cruz del Carmen. Car tour 4
🚌 1.705 to Las Carboneras

Follow *Alternative* walk 19 (page 100) to Las Escaleras, a viewpoint overlooking two valleys. Easy climb and descent of 100m/330ft. Shade nearby.

19c LAS CARBONERAS (map on reverse of touring map) ○

by car or taxi: 20-30min on foot *by bus: 20-30min on foot*
🚗 Las Carboneras: the road is 1km east of Cruz del Carmen. Car tour 4
🚌 1.705 to Las Carboneras

From bus stop/car park follow the road (gravel at the time of writing) towards Chinamada. You will come to the best views after about 30 minutes, where there is a lone farmhouse off on your right. No shade.

Guajara and the Chapel of the Snows (Picnic 10)

20 NEAR TABORNO (map on reverse of touring map, photograph page 102) ○

by car or taxi: 25-30min on foot *by bus: 25-30min on foot*
🚗 Taborno: the road is 1km east of Cruz del Carmén. Car tour 4
🚌 1.705 to Taborno
Follow Walk 20 from the 1h10min-point (Taborno, page 104) to the viewpoint reached in 25min. No shade.

21 NEAR CASA NEGRÍN (map on reverse of touring map, photographs page 104, 113)

by car or taxi: 5-10min on foot *by bus: 5-10min on foot*
🚗 at the restaurant Casa Negrín (take the Las Carboneras road, 1km east of Cruz del Carmén; then take the first right turn off the road). Car tour 4
🚌 1.705; ask to be put off at Casa Negrín
Follow Walk 21 (page 106) to the cottage overlooking the Afur Valley.

22 BARRANCO DE TAHODIO (map on reverse of touring map)

by car or taxi: 20-25min on foot *by bus: 30-35min on foot*
🚗 Mirador Pico del Inglés. Car tours 2, 4
🚌 1705, 1.706, 1.708 or 1.710 to the Pico del Inglés turn-off
Follow Walk 22 (page 110) to the lookout point over the *barranco* and dam. There are also views to El Teide. The path is shown on page 110. Tiring climb to return.

23 NEAR TAGANANA (map on reverse of touring map, photograph page 114) ○

by car or taxi: 50min on foot *by bus: 50min on foot*
🚗 Taganana. Car tour 2 🚌 246 to Taganana
Follow Walk 23 (page 112), to picnic anywhere after the turn-off for Afur. Overlooks the village and the valley. No shade. Climb and descent of 150m/500ft.

24a ANAGA FORESTRY PARK (map reverse of touring map) ⛩

by car or taxi: up to 5min on foot *by bus: not easily accessible*
🚗 forestry park, on the TF1123, east of El Bailadero. Car tour 2
Shade of laurels. Full *zona recreativa* facilities (see page 10). A nearby setting is shown on page 117.

24b CHINOBRE (map on reverse of touring map)

by car or taxi: 35min on foot *by bus: not easily accessible*
🚗 forestry park, on the TF1123, east of El Bailadero. Car tour 2
Follow Walk 24 from the 2h-point (the forestry park) to the Chinobre *mirador* — one of the best viewpoints on Tenerife. Shade of laurels. A nearby setting is shown on page 117.

24c PLAYA DE BENIJO (map on reverse of touring map) ○

by car or taxi: 5-10min on foot *by bus: 20-25min on foot*
near the beach, 4km past Taganana on the TF1124. Car tour 2
246; ask to be put off at the Almáciga turn-off and walk east to the beach.

Beautiful coastal views. The only shade is from the cliffs. The coast at nearby Almáciga is shown on page 18.

25a LAS CASILLAS (map on reverse of touring map, photograph page 118) ○

by car or taxi: 40min on foot *by bus: not easily accessible*
off the TF1123: about 10km east of El Bailadero, there should be a small yellow sign for 'Igueste' on the right-hand side of the road, pointing down a path. This is just *before* a sharp bend in the road. Just *past* the sign (still on the bend in the road) there is a forestry track on the right, where you should park. If the sign is still missing, you can find the track and path if you navigate *very carefully:* use the large-scale map on the reverse of the touring map. Car tour 2

After parking, walk west along the road and watch for a path down on your left. Pick up Walk 25 at the 3h40min-point to reach Las Casillas, from where you overlook Igueste and its ravine. The descent and re-ascent is steep for about 10 minutes.

25b BARRANCO DE UJANA (map on reverse of touring map)

by car or taxi: up to 10min on foot *by bus: not easily accessible*
as Picnic 25a above. Car tour 2

After parking (as above) walk west along the road for two minutes: watch for a path climbing on your right, through cultivation and trees. Continue up to a stream. Good shade, but the stream is dry in mid-summer.

26 CHAMORGA OVERLOOK (map on reverse of touring map) ○

by car or taxi: 15-20min on foot *by bus: not easily accessible*
Chamorga: a suggested detour from Las Bodegas, the 68km-point in Car tour 2 (pages 22-23)

From the village square, keep left, rounding the hillside, to come to the bar/shop. From here follow a path up behind and to the left of the bar, to the top of the ridge overlooking the village and its ravine. No shade. Steep, short climb of about 100m/330ft.

27 IGUESTE (map on reverse of touring map, photograph page 120) ○

by car or taxi: 5-10min on foot *by bus: 5-10min on foot*
Igueste, on the TF1121. Car tour 2 245 to Igueste

East of the bridge in the *barranco,* continue down the path to the rocky beach. No shade. Coastal views. Pleasant spot.

Touring

Car hire on the island is good value. *Do* shop around; hire prices vary considerably. Examine the car before you take it on the road, and make certain that the applicable motoring laws and insurance information are given to you in writing *in English.*

The car tours are numbered in order of importance: if you will only tour for a day or two, there is no question about priorities. Don't miss Tour 1!

Car tour 1: You could stretch your legs with a short walk to the Piedras Amarillas (Picnic 11, Walks 8 and 11)

The touring notes are brief: they include little history or information readily available in standard guides or in free leaflets obtainable from the tourist offices. The facilities and 'sights' of the towns are not described for this same reason. Instead, I concentrate on the 'logistics' of touring: times and distances, road conditions, and seeing some of 'hidden' Tenerife. Most of all, I emphasise possibilities for **walking** and **picnicking** (the symbol ***P*** alerts you to a picnic spot; see pages 10-16). While some of the references to picnics 'off the beaten track' may not be suitable during a long car tour, you may see a landscape that you would like to explore at leisure another day, when you have more time.

The large touring map is designed to be held out opposite the touring notes and contains all the information you will need outside the towns. The tours have been written up with Puerto as departure/return point, but can easily be joined from other centres. Plans of Puerto de la Cruz and Santa Cruz, with city exits, are on pages 8 and 9.

Take along warm clothing and some **food and drink**: you may experience delays, especially on mountainous roads. **Allow plenty of time for stops**: the times given for the tours include only brief stops at viewpoints labelled (📷) in the notes. **Telephones** are located in most villages. WC is used to indicate public toilets; others are found at restaurants.

Distances quoted are *cumulative km* ***from Puerto.*** *A* key to the symbols in the notes is on the touring map. **All motorists should read the country code on page 37 and go quietly in the countryside. *Buen viage!***

Almáciga, perched above the coast (Car tour 2, Walks 24, 26)

1 THE OROTAVA VALLEY AND LAS CAÑADAS

Puerto de la Cruz • La Orotava • Las Cañadas • Los Gigantes • Guía de Isora • Adeje • Playa de las Américas • Playa de los Cristianos • Vilaflor • Las Cañadas • Puerto de la Cruz

244km/151mi; 7-8h driving; Exit B from Puerto (plan pages 8-9)

En route: ⛩ at La Caldera, Montaña Alta, Las Cañadas road, Chio, Las Lajas; Picnics (see ***P*** symbol and pages 10-17): 2, 4, 5a, 5b, 7a-g, 10, 11, (12a), 12b; Walks 1-12

This long excursion requires a very early start. *Don't be put off by dark clouds over the north, because very often Las Cañadas and the south are soaking up the sunshine! All roads are in good condition.*

Photographs of the tour on pages 17, 21, 23, 51, 59, 60, 63, 64, 66-67, 68-69, 72, 75

This dramatic circuit begins gently, in the lush Orotava Valley. Wind your way up into the pines on the higher slopes and soon the landscape changes abruptly: you cross the vast, bare plateau of the Las Cañadas crater. Fields of jagged scoria layer the floor with the occasional sprinkling of *retama,* a hardy broom. Southward, heading towards the coast, some calmness returns to the landscape, as smooth mounds of the more recent volcanoes emerge. Picturesque villages set on the severe southern escarpments remind you of the other side of Tenerife — a more sombre beauty.

Leave Puerto via the motorway (Avenida de Colón) and follow the C821 through **La Orotava★** (7km ✝✕ ⛽⊕).* The road (⛽) continues uphill past the turn-off to Benijos (for ***P***12a at Changjiga; ⛩). Old lichen-covered walls hide well-tilled plots, and scatterings of aged chestnut trees line the route to **Aguamansa** and the **trout farm** (20km ✕WC***P***5b), where Walks 1-3 begin and Walk 5 ends. Just after, turn left to **La Caldera★** (22km ✕⛩WC ***P***4, 5a). This tiny crater, where Walks 4-6 begin and Walk 7 ends, is a superb viewpoint over the green Orotava slopes and down to the sea. From here keep climbing (📷), past the famous Margarita de Piedra★, a rock shaped like a daisy (see page 12), and several roadside picnic areas (⛩; ***P***2, 7b-g).

*As this is a very long tour and La Orotava is so close to Puerto, save your visit for another day. The town is best seen during the festival of Corpus Christi (May/June): the streets are carpeted in flowers, and in the main square intriguingly-beautiful religious 'paintings' are made from the multi-coloured sands of Las Cañadas. Visit Calle de San Francisco, with its magnificent old mansions, lovely courtyards and wooden balconies. Also of interest are the main church (La Concepción, 18C, the botanical gardens, and the church of San Juán, which commands a superb view of the Orotava Valley.

Walks 7, 8 and 12 begin at **El Portillo** (39km WC***P***7a, 12b), where the nearby **Cañadas Visitors' Information Centre** welcomes you to 'another planet' — **Las Cañadas★**. The constant change in colour and rock formation within the encircling crater walls is the highlight of this tour — and, I imagine, of your visit. Sharp streams of rock give way to smooth mounds of pumice and fine scoria, while sunken sea-beds of gravel create 'pools' along the floor. The majestic El Teide is with you wherever you go, and Montaña de Guajara, rising out of the encircling wall like an abutment, rivals El Teide in beauty.

The leisurely drive through this wonderland () takes you past the turn-off to Montaña Blanca and El Teide (Walk 9) and finally brings you to the **Parador de las Cañadas** (52km ***P***11) and the **Roques de García** (***P***10), a troupe of rocky upthrusts overlooking the vast Ucanca Plain. Walks 10 and 11 begin and end here. Barely a kilometre further on, you'll be intrigued by the patches of iron-containing blue rock in the embankment at the side of the road ('Los Azulejos') — even more striking when seen from the plain below.

At the pass of **Boca de Tauce** (59km) fork right on the C823 for 'Isora'. For several kilometres, the road cuts its way through the dark lava flows. Pines reappear, scattered across the landscape, and smooth volcanic cones remind you of the last volcanic outbursts. Set amidst this scenery is the lovely Chio *zona recreativa* (). Past here, the Las Estrellas restaurant () is a good viewing point over the southwest coast.

Leave the C823 at a junction (89km) and continue to the right, along the C820 towards Santiago del Teide. At **Tamaimo** (93km), an attractive village sheltering below a high rocky protrusion, turn left on the TF6281. Tomato plants now cover the landscape as the route winds down to Los Gigantes. At the 99km- mark, at a junction, keep right for Puerto de Santiago. **Los Gigantes** (101km) is a modern tourist complex, set below sheer cliffs★ rising vertically out of the sea. From Los Gigantes make for tiny **Puerto de Santiago** () and then join the TF6237 via the sandy beach of La Arena. The next village on the route is tranquil **San Juán** (113km).

From San Juán head up the TF623 to **Guía de Isora** (123km ⊕), a small country town sitting on bare rock slopes. Stretch your legs here and wander down a

The coast below the Orotava Valley (Car tour 1)

couple of the quaint old streets. Then continue on the street through the centre of town; it leads you up a narrow lane and onto the C822: turn right. **Adeje** (138km) lies off the main road (at the turn-off), resting below crags and a table-topped mountain in the background. The great chasm, the Barranco del Infierno★, runs past the edge of the village. Take the shady tree-lined street out of Adeje, to return to the C822.

Now you have a choice of fine sandy beaches. **Playa de las Américas**, a lively, modern holiday resort with everything going 'in top gear', is only a minute off the C822 (147km ⊕WC). **Playa de los Cristianos**, 1.5km off the main road (149km ⊕WC), is somewhat smaller and less lively.

From the beaches head inland again via Arona (the old C822 and TF511). **Arona** (158km) has a charming shady church square, surrounded by balconied old houses. It overlooks the sparkling greenhouses on the lowlands. Vineyards on walled slopes surround the TF5112 to **Vilaflor** (172km ⊕), the highest town on Tenerife at 1161m/3810ft. Nestled on the edge of a plain, this mountain settlement looks up onto the steep, forested inclines that run down off the high mountain spurs above. From Vilaflor follow the C821 back to Las Cañadas, passing some of the loveliest Canary pine forests on the island. Los Pinos, a *mirador* 2km past Vilaflor, sits amidst these regal ancient pines (). The road takes you through some spectacular rugged mountain landscapes (at 178km, Las Lajas *zona recreativa;* at 183km).

You re-enter the crater at Boca de Tauce (189km). The twisted uprising of rock here is more impressive when approached from the south. Bear right along the C821 and return to Puerto under the late afternoon sun. The mood of Las Cañadas changes under this soft light. Shadows fall across the crater floor, colours mellow, and low clouds begin curling over the crater walls, as you retrace your outgoing route to Puerto (244km).

2 THE RUGGED ANAGA PENINSULA

Puerto de la Cruz • Pico del Inglés • Roque Negro • El Bailadero • Las Bodegas • (Chamorga) • Taganana • Almáciga • Benijo • San Andrés • Igueste • Puerto

171km/106mi; 5-6h driving; Exit B from Puerto (plan pages 8-9)

En route: ⛩ at the Anaga Forestry Park; Picnics (see ***P*** symbol and pages 10-17): 22-27; Walks 21-27

Driving is slow in this mountainous terrain, but the roads are not busy. Fill up with petrol before starting out; there are no petrol stations in the Anaga, and none on the touring route until San Andrés. ***Hint:*** *Beyond Las Mercedes, refer to the large-scale map of the Anaga on the reverse of the touring map.*

Photographs of the tour on pages 18, 104, 113, 114, 120

This excursion takes you amidst the mountains of the Anaga Peninsula. Twisting along the backbone of this range, the road is one continuous *mirador.* Inland, lost in these rugged contours, lie tiny remote villages, clinging to rocky nodules. And along the coast, quiet and secluded little bays unravel.

Take the motorway (TF5, ⛽) towards Santa Cruz, but leave it at the Guamasa exit. From Guamasa take the TF820 towards La Laguna, then follow the signposting for Las Mercedes (TF121, ⛽). Beyond the well-settled plain join the TF114, immersing yourself in the coolness of the laurel forest. Pass the Mirador Cruz del Carmen (📷) and the turn-off to Las Carboneras (Tour 4).

Pico del Inglés★ is your first stop. Turn right off the road to this fabulous *mirador* with its far-reaching views (40km 📷***P***22). Walk 22 begins here. Then head back 1km and turn right on the main road (now numbered TF1123). Solitary houses speckle the ridges segmenting the isolated Afur valley. Some 3km along, turn left to **Roque Negro** (TF1127), a small village overshadowed by an enormous black basalt rock (47km 📷). The village square serves as a good look-out point: Afur can be seen far below in the shadows of these high crests and the beach, the Playa del Tamadite, lies beyond the village. This is the setting for Walk 21, which ends at Roque Negro. Return to the TF1123 and turn left.

At the 57km-mark, turn off left for **El Bailadero★** (📷✕), where Walks 24 and 25 begin. Some 5km further on come to the lovely **Anaga Forestry Park** and *zona recreativa* (⛩***P***24a, 24b) — a better place to start Walks 24 and 25, if friends will play chauffeur. The road is flanked by a dense laurel forest. At the **Mirador de las Chamucadas** (63km 📷), you'll have good views down to Igueste, a superbly-sited village visited later.

Descending in S-bends into open rocky terrain (**P**25a and 25b), come into **Las Bodegas** (68km), sheltered in a narrow *barranco.* La Cumbrilla, on the ridge above, is more impressive because of its surroundings. (If you don't mind bumpy roads, make a 6km return detour now to Chamorga (**P**26), one of Tenerife's most beautiful villages. Barely a minute up the road from Las Bodegas, turn right and pass under Cumbrilla (through a tunnel) and head down into Chamorga. A smattering of white dwellings, the hamlet snuggles into the sides of a *barranco,* shaded by palms and loquat trees. Walk 26, only accessible by car, begins and ends here.)

The main tour returns from Las Bodegas to the Taganana turn-off on the *left.* Some 2km downhill, turn left again. After passing through a tunnel under the Bailadero *mirador,* you overlook the rural wonders of the Taganana. This stretch of escarpment is a landscape of razor-sharp ridges cutting down to the sea. **Taganana★** (89km ✝✕⊕**P**23), where Walk 23 begins, is a brilliant array of white houses spread across the lower crests. The palms gracing the gardens make this settlement extremely photogenic. Roque de las Animas (the Ghosts' Rock) towers straight above the road 1km beyond the village. **Playa del Roque★** (91km ✕), with its roadside bars, is a pleasant refreshment stop-off. Past **Almáciga, Benijo** (**P**24c), where the tar ends, is but a few cottages and a beach. (From here a gravel road continues to isolated El Draguillo; Alternative walk 24.)

Retracing your route through the tunnel, follow the TF112 down the Barranco de San Andrés to the south coast. From **San Andrés** (114km ✕⛽), turn left for Igueste. Just outside San Andrés, the palms of **Las Teresitas** (Tenerife's only white-sand beach) add a touch of the tropics. You'll catch glimpses of other tiny sandy bays, barely visible from the road, as you approach serene **Igueste** (120km **P**27), one of my favourite villages. Walk 27 begins and ends here. From Igueste the TF1121 and TF111 take you to Santa Cruz, where you pick up the motorway (⛽) for Puerto (171km).

Car tour 1: a colourful setting typical of the Orotava Valley

3 SPECTACULAR NORTHWEST SETTINGS

Puerto de la Cruz • San Juán de la Rambla • Icod de los Vinos • Garachico • Punta de Teno • Santiago del Teide • La Montañeta • Icod el Alto • Puerto de la Cruz

145km/90mi; 6-7h driving; Exit A from Puerto (plan pages 8-9)

En route: ⛩ at El Lagar and Las Arenas Negras; Picnics (see ***P*** symbol and pages 10-17): (13), 14, 16-18; Walks 13, 14, (15), 16-18

Except for the C820, the roads are narrow and winding. Some people may find the road between Masca and Santiago vertiginous.

Photographs of the tour on pages 25, 26, 79, 92, 93

A backdrop embroidered in greens highlights the small and picturesque villages, precipitous sunken valleys, superb coastal settings and sheer shadowy peaks that characterise the landscapes visited on this circuit.

Head west from Puerto on the C820. This coastal road passes below cliffs towering up to the left, while breakers crash below on the right. **San Juán de la Rambla** (16km) is a charming, fresh-white village overlooking the sea. Las Aguas, a neighbouring hamlet on the rocky shoreline below, is a picture-postcard scene glimpsed just before San Juán. All the way from Puerto to the northwestern tip of the island, you're immersed in banana palms and bright seasonal blooms.

Continuing along the C820, come into **Icod de los Vinos** (26km ✝⛰✕⛽⊕), on the fertile vine-growing slopes below El Teide. The 16th/17th-century San Marcos Church merits a visit. Just below the lovely church square is Icod's famous ancient dragon tree. The nearby Playa de San Marcos is a small sandy beach surrounded by dark jagged cliffs (a 5km return detour).

Manorial homes amidst banana plantations come into view as you leave Icod on the TF142, hugging the coast. Come into **Garachico★** (32km ✝⛰✕⛽⊕). This beautifully-situated village, once an important port, was destroyed by a volcanic eruption in the early 18th century. But a few buildings of interest survive: the 16th-century San Miguel Castle, the Baroque palace of the Marqués de Adeje, the 17th-century Convent of San Francisco, and the Church of Santa Ana (founded in 1548). Garachico is otherwise known for its inviting natural rock pools. The Roque de Garachico, rising up off the shore, bears a cross to protect the little town from another catastrophe.

Continuing west on the TF142 (⛽), the village of **Buenavista** (40km ✕⛽⊕) is seen up ahead, resting on a fertile coastal plain, walled in by high sharp crags. Walk 18 and Alternative walk 17 end here. Gorges and

The famous dragon tree at Icod de los Vinos (Car tour 3)

valleys cut back into this cataclysm of rocks. At the first junction, turn right and then immediately left, following signs for the 'Faro de Teno'. Three kilometres along the TF1429 there are especially fine views from the **Punta del Fraile** (📷***P***18), where the island falls away into an indigo sea. The road continues to wind its way around and under rough indented cliffs, high above the sea, and then descends to the lighthouse on the dark volcanic promontory of **Punta de Teno** (48km 📷). This is one of the richest botanical areas in the Canaries. From here return to Buenavista (56km): at the junction, turn right on the TF1426 for El Palmar.

El Palmar's valley lies well hidden above the coastal plain. A steep climb through rocky terrain covered in prickly pear, *vinagrera* and wild geraniums leads up past magnificently-terraced slopes. Pass **El Palmar** (62km), where Walk 17 ends. Walk 18 begins just a little further along the road. Then, almost at once, come to fabulous views over charming **Masca** (68km ✕📷), a fovourite village among the islanders.

At **Santiago del Teide** (73km ✝✕⛽⊕) you rejoin the C820, heading north towards Icod de los Vinos. A great change takes place as you leave Santiago's treeless valley and enter the green slopes above **Erjos** (***P***17), where Walk 16 can end and Walk 17 begins. This rough countryside soon gives way to cultivated plots of vegetables and fruit trees. Pass through **El Tanque** (86km ⛽) and soon come to the **Mirador de Garachico** (88km 📷✕), from where you'll have the best outlook over the village setting and the off-shore rock.

At 91km, about 3km past the *mirador*, turn right for 'El Amparo, La Vega' (TF2225). At a junction just under 4km up, turn right and, almost immediately after, right again. These are the slopes that produce Icod's well-known wines. Pass **La Vega**, where Walk 15 ends, before reaching **La Montañeta** (100km ⊼***P***16), sitting comfortably in a hollow at the edge of the pines. Walk 16 begins here. Returning along the same road, your views stretch down the escarpment and out along the eastern coastline. Follow the signs for El Amparo.

(If you have time for an 8km return detour and don't mind a steep, narrow and bumpy road, Redondo might appeal to you. The turn-off *(not signposted)* is about 6km downhill from La Montañeta: it's a right-hand turning just *past* a house and *before a* sharp bend in the road; the street is signed 'La Petita'. The area has unique stone cottages — several tiny dwellings glued into one, and each room has its own separate roof!)

The main tour continues back to Icod de los Vinos (109km) where, at a junction, you turn left and then right, to rejoin the C820. Your next turn-off is 3km up the road on the right: a steady climb on the TF222 through rocky farmland leads to **La Guancha** (119km ✗⛽⊕***P***14), where Walk 14 ends and Alternative walk 15-3 begins. Troughs full of scarlet geraniums brighten up the streets. (Past here, another 6km return detour is highly recommended: 6km past La Guancha, turn right up an unmarked road, just before Icod el Alto. In 3km you'll come to the La Corona *mirador* (✗📷***P***13), overlooking the magnificent Orotava Valley.) The main tour continues straight along the TF221 to another farming area set on steep slopes, **Icod el Alto** (126km 📷), where Walks 13 and 14 begin.

Rounding the escarpment and leaving the village, the road, cut into the sheer rock face, affords tremendous views on the descent into the Orotava Valley. The TF213 takes you through upper and lower Los Realejos (⛰✗⛽⊕ and oldest ✝ on Tenerife) and returns you to the C820. Continue east to regain Puerto after 145km.

The mountains of Teno, with El Palmar in the valley (Car tour 3, near Walk 17)

4 QUIET CORNERS OF THE ANAGA

Puerto de la Cruz • Tacoronte • Mesa del Mar • Bajamar • Punta del Hidalgo • Las Carboneras • Taborno • Pico del Inglés • La Laguna • Puerto de la Cruz

122km/76mi; 5h driving; Exit B from Puerto (plan pages 8-9)

En route: Picnics (see ***P*** symbol and pages 10-17): 19-22; Walks 19-23

This can be an afternoon's drive, but it's better to spend a leisurely day over it: driving will be slow on the narrow winding roads. The descent to Mesa del Mar is down a precipitous rock face, and might be unnerving for some people. ***Hint:*** *Beyond Las Canteras, refer to the large-scale map of the Anaga on the reverse of the touring map.*

Photographs of the tour on pages 28, 102, 104, 113 and cover

Drive down to the coast and take a dip in the seawater pools (there are several choices), continue up to the summits of the Anaga and go for a stroll in the laurel forest, then perhaps finish the day on a cultural note: saunter around the streets of La Laguna.

Take the motorway (TF5) from Puerto as far as the turn-off for El Sauzal. From here, follow the signs (C820) for **Tacoronte** (15km ✝⛰✕⛽⊕). The wooden statue of Christ in the 17th-century church here is attributed with numerous miracles and is revered by many of the islanders. Leave Tacoronte on the TF1221 (signposted for Valle Guerra). Some 4km along, turn left for 'Mesa del Mar'. At a junction 1km down, keep straight ahead. A descent past large houses with gardens full of colour brings you to the cliffs overlooking the precipitous coastline. The tourist complex of **Mesa del Mar** lies below, on jagged rocks jutting out into the sea. Superb coastal views unfold as you descend this steep, convoluted road (📷). The complex itself is of little interest but, behind it, through a tunnel, you'll find a sandy beach below the sheer cliffs.

Return to the TF1221 and turn left for **Valle Guerra** (25km ⛽). From there follow signs for **Tejina** (31km ✕⛽), then join the TF121 for Bajamar. Colourfully-blooming bushes and creepers, together with large banana plantations, enliven the landscape along here. The village's tidal pools make **Bajamar★** (34km ⛰✕⛽⊕) a popular resort and swimming spot. Sharp ridges descend behind the settlement, but plants in all shades of green soothe the dark, abrupt inclines. Continue on the same road to **Punta del Hidalgo★** (37km ⛰✕📷***P***19a). It lies across a slight bay with a rocky beach, across from Bajamar. The road ends past the village, at a roundabout where high craggy crests fall into the sea. Walk 19 sets out from here (see cover photograph).

The Anaga Peninsula at Bajamar (Car tour 4)

Return to Tejina, then continue on the TF121 to **Tegueste** (49km ✕⛽). These two small villages on grassy inclines open your way up to **Las Canteras** (55km), where you turn left on the TF114 and head up into the magnificent laurel forest. A *mirador* (📷) on the right, 3km from Las Canteras, gives you captivating views of the lush green undulating hills outside La Laguna. Then reach **Cruz del Carmen★** (59km ✕📷), a well-designed viewpoint, framed by the forest. From here you overlook the Aguere Valley of La Laguna and have more views of the ever-present Teide.

For a brief time you leave the thick of the forest, as you drive down to the two beautifully-situated villages of Las Carboneras and Taborno: 1km past Cruz del Carmen turn left on the TF1145. Pass the turn-off to Casa Negrín (✕*P*21), where Walk 20 ends and Walk 21 begins. Valleys open up as you descend, and Punta del Hidalgo reveals itself for a moment. The Roque de Taborno is a prominent landmark sitting high atop the ridge. **Las Carboneras★** (67km ✕*P*19b, 19c) sits glued to a hill, encircled by cultivation. Walks 19 and 23 end here; Walk 20 starts out here. Now return to the road (TF1128) passed earlier and turn left. After descending a forested ridge, you come into **Taborno★** (72km 📷 *P*20), where small dwellings are dispersed along the crest of the ridge, rising high above two deep *barrancos.* Walks 20 and 23 both pass through the hamlet.

Returning to the main road (now numbered TF1123), turn left. After 1km come to the turn-off right for the *mirador* **Pico del Inglés★** (81km 📷*P*22). Perched on the spine of this range that divides the island north and south, the *mirador* offers views down into the hidden cultivation of the Afur Valley, captures snippets of the coast, and looks out towards the island's guardian, El Teide. Walk 22 descends from here to Santa Cruz. From Pico del Inglés make for the charming university town of **La Laguna** on the TF114 and TF121, before returning to Puerto (122km).

5 THE SUN-BAKED SOUTH

Puerto de la Cruz • El Portillo • Güimar • Arico • La Candelaria • Puerto de la Cruz

234km/145mi; 6h driving; Exit B from Puerto (plan pages 8-9)

En route: ⛩ at the *zonas recreativas* either side of the Mirador Pico de las Flores on the C824; Picnics (see ***P*** symbol and pages 10-17): 6, 7a, 12b; Walks 6, 7, 8, 12

Generally good driving, except for 30km of bumpy, narrow road between Fasnia and Arico. The motorways are always busy. Part of the C824 (between La Esperanza and the Arafo turn-off) is often enshrouded in low-lying mists. Note that there are no petrol stations en route between La Esperanza and Güimar — more than 70km.

Photographs of the tour on pages 54-55, 59, 75

From the greenest to the driest, from the lowest to the highest, and from forested to naked — this drive has it all. The higher inclines along the southern flanks of the island, missed by most tourists, are a dramatic contrast to the rich green slopes of the north.

Leave Puerto by Exit B and zip along the motorway (⛽) to La Laguna, where this tour *really* starts. At the turn-off for La Laguna (28km), head right on the C824. Lush green pasturelands lie along your way to **La Esperanza** (33km ✂⛽), as you ascend the spine of the island. Beyond La Esperanza, eucalyptus and pines forest the crest. From this vantage point, you have a number of *miradors* and two picnic sites. The first *mirador,* **Pico de las Flores** (39km 📷⛩), overlooks the luxuriant slopes down to Santa Cruz and up to the Anaga range. Another viewpoint (📷) lies a kilometre further up. Next is **Mirador Ortuño** (📷), with views to the pine-robed slopes of El Teide. A detour of 1km is required for the Mirador de Cumbres (📷), which also looks out over the northern slopes.

La Crucita (60km 📷*P*6) is the point where pilgrims cross the C824 on their way from the north to Candelaria. Walk 6 follows this ancient route. As you near the pass at the top of the road, the pines subside and rocky protrusions, covered in *retama,* take over the landscape. Later the terrain changes again, as rich volcanic tones — maroons, purples, russets, wines, greys and blacks — flow in and out of each other.

El Portillo (73km ✂WC⛩*P*7a, 12b) is the starting point for Walks 7, 8 and 12. Here you turn round and head back along the C824, for the descent to the southern slopes. Arafo, your next centre, is not signposted from this direction, and *the turn-off is easily missed:* it's 20km from El Portillo (93km on the circuit);

turn down right. Pines accompany you partway on this descent but, as you approach the lower slopes, loose scatterings of chestnuts take over. The Güimar basin opens up ahead, revealing corners with great ravines cutting back deep into the steep escarpment (97km). High brown stone terraces step the slopes of this productive agricultural centre. Vineyards, interplanted with vegetables, cover the greater part of the land. Bypass the centre of Arafo (where Walk 6 ends) and continue straight on through **Güimar** (115km).

Come out onto the old C822 and head towards Fasnia. This bumpy old road winds in and out of shallow ravines before climbing out of the basin along the eastern escarpment. The **Mirador de D Martin** (121km) offers you a final view of this great valley. From here on, the monotone landscape becomes more harsh. Trees have vanished, save for the fine-branched Jerusalem thorn bordering the roadside. In April and November, its yellow blossoms cheer up this countryside. Rock walls terrace the slopes. You'll notice, too, masses of roadside caves — squared, arched, and with doors or gates. Often the doorways open into enormous chambers. The coastline is always within sight below.

Fasnia (133km) is a pleasant country village set back off the road. Between here and Arico there are few settlements, and the land is not under cultivation. At **Arico** (148km), turn left on the TF613 and make your way back down to the motorway (TF1), then head left for Santa Cruz. After 23km turn off to **La Candelaria★** (179km). The basilica (1958) houses the new statue of Nuestra Señora de la Candelaria, the island's patron saint. (The original statue was supposedly found in 1390 by Guanche herdsmen and was lost in a tidal wave in 1826.) The large square on the seafront near the modern church is quite impressive, with red-rock statues representing Tenerife's ten former Guanche chiefs (see title page). From here follow the motorways to Puerto (234km). As you re-enter the Orotava Valley, the tapestry of greens and browns, sprinkled with white settlements and crowned by the majesty of El Teide, comes into full view.

El Draguillo (Walk 24; Alternative walk 26)

Walking

This book covers most of the best walking on Tenerife — enough ground to keep even the most energetic hiker going for a good month. While all the best walks in the popular Orotava Valley have been included, please try not to miss other rambles around the island, especially on the Teno and Anaga peninsulas.

I hope you will also use this book, together with the bus timetables on pages 128-132, to make up your own walk combinations. I've indicated where routes link up on the walking maps, and the fold-out touring map shows the general location of all the walks. One word of caution: **Never try to get from one walk to another on uncharted terrain!** Only link up walks by following paths described in these notes or by using roads or tracks. Do not try to cross rough country (which might prove dangerous) or private land (where you might not have right of way).

There are walks in the book for everyone.

Beginners: Start on the walks graded 'easy', and be sure to look at all the short and alternative walks — some are easy versions of the long walks. You need look no further than the picnic suggestions on pages 10 to 16 to find a large selection of *very* easy rambles.

Experienced walkers: If you are used to rough terrain

and have a head for heights, you should be able to tackle all the walks in the book, *except those recommended* ***for experts only***. Of course, you must take into account the season and weather conditions. For example, in rainy weather some of the *barranco* walks will be unsuitable; in strong winds or snow do not plan excursions to the mountains! And, always remember that **storm damage can make these routes unsafe at any time!** Remember, too: always follow the route as described in this book. If you have not reached one of the landmarks after a reasonable time, you must go back to the last 'sure' point and start again.

Experts: Provided that you are used to sheer, unprotected drops and scree, you don't mind finding your own routes where necessary, *and provided that conditions are still as described in the notes,* you should be able to tackle all the walks in the book.

Guides, waymarking, maps

Guides are not easily found on Tenerife, but you can enquire at a tourist information office or ask your tour rep, as well as looking in the tourist newspapers. You might also enquire at the Hotel Tigaiga, where group walking tours are often organised for the (mainly German) clientele who visit the hotel; don't worry, the guides speak English as well as German.

Waymarking is good in the Orotava Valley and on some Anaga walks, thanks to the efforts of ICONA and the island government. But, as they warn you in their walks leaflets, **never walk without a map!**

The **maps** in this book have been very greatly adapted from the 1:25,000 military maps of the island. Most have been reprinted at a scale of 1:40,000, but a few are at a smaller scale: *be sure to check the scale on the map!* You can purchase the military maps on Tenerife (enquire at the government offices in Santa Cruz, No 2 on the town plan), but do remember that they are not up-to-date, and some of the paths they show are no longer viable.

Dogs — and other nuisances

Dogs will be the only real worry you may encounter on your walks. They're usually small and noisy, but the sight of a stick sends them scurrying. However, if you do a lot of walking on the island, you are bound to meet at least one unfriendly monster, rightly guarding his territory. You may wish to invest in a 'Dog Dazer', an ultrasonic device which frightens dogs off without harming them. For information write to Dazer UK, 51 Alfriston Road, London SW11 6NR.

Hunters may startle you with bursts of gunfire, but they present no other worries. They come out in force on the weekends and on holidays — always trailed by yapping dogs.

Give chained **billy goats** a wide berth; they don't like intruders! Other than that, you've no other pests to worry you on Tenerife — there are no poisonous snakes or insects.

ICONA's helpful signposting is especially in evidence in the Orotava Valley and on the Anaga Peninsula.

What to take

If you're already on Tenerife when you find this book, and you haven't any special equipment such as a rucksack or walking boots, you can still so some of the walks — or buy yourself some equipment at one of the sports shops. *Don't* attempt the more difficult walks without the proper gear. For each walk in the book, the *minimum year-round equipment* is listed. Where walking boots are required, there is no substitute: you will need to rely on the grip and ankle support they provide, as well as their waterproof qualities. All other walks should be done with stout lace-up shoes with thick rubber soles, to grip on wet, slippery surfaces.

You may find the following checklist useful:

walking boots (which *must* be broken-in and comfortable)
waterproof rain gear (outside summer months)
long-sleeved shirt (sun protection)
first-aid kit, including bandages, plasters and antiseptic cream
plastic plates, cups, etc
anorak (zip opening)
spare bootlaces
sunhat, sunglasses, suncream
whistle, compass, torch
up-to-date bus timetables (see page 7)
plastic bottle with water purifying tablets
long trousers, tight at the ankles
knives and openers
2 lightweight cardigans
extra pair of socks
plastic groundsheet
small rucksack
insect repellent
Dog Dazer (see under 'Dogs')

Please bear in mind that I've not done *every* walk in this book under *all* weather conditions; use your judgement to modify the list according to the season.

Walkers' checklist

The following points cannot be stressed too often:

- **At any time a walk may become unsafe due to storm damage or bulldozing.** If the route is not as described in this book, and your way ahead is not secure, do not attempt to go on.
- **Walks for experts only** may be unsuitable in winter, and all mountain walks may be hazardous then.
- **Never walk alone** — four is the best walking group. If someone is injured, two can go for help, and there will be no need for panic in an emergency.
- **Do not overestimate your energies**: your speed will be determined by the slowest walker in the group.
- **Bus** connections at the end of a walk may be vital.
- **Proper shoes or boots** are a necessity.
- **Mists** can suddenly appear on the higher elevations.
- **Warm clothing** is needed in the mountains; even in summer take some along, in case you are delayed.
- **First-aid kit, compass, whistle, torch** weigh little, but might save your life.
- **Extra rations** must be taken on long walks.
- **Always take a sunhat with you**, and in summer a cover-up for your arms and legs as well.
- Read and re-read the important note on page 2, the country code on page 37, and the guidelines on grade and equipment for each walk you plan.

Where to stay

For walkers **Puerto de la Cruz** is the best base. Attractive Puerto has an efficient bus service and a wide choice of accommodation. Most of the walks described are easily accessible from here; the remainder require a few bus changes (making for long days, but little inconvenience). However, recognising that **the south** has become the major tourist centre, the bus timetables include some important connections from the Playas. Consider spending one or two nights in the solitary and peaceful **Parador de las Cañadas**. You can book in advance: Parador Nacional de las Cañadas del Teide, Santa Cruz, Tenerife; or telephone: 922/38 64 15. If you're adventurous, you could also stay at the refuge on El Teide: contact your local tourist office for information and the necessary permission. Finally, if you're not tied into 'package' accommodation, note that there are hotels in La Laguna and Santa Cruz, bringing you closer to the Anaga walks — *which you must not miss!*

Weather hints

Island weather is often unpredictable, but there are a few signs and weather patterns that may help you forecast a walking day.

Tenerife is blessed with year-round walking weather. The north, unfortunately, has more than its fair share of rain, but rests under pleasant temperatures. The south soaks up the sun. Wind strikes the southern coastline east of Los Cristianos, but rain is a rarity.

Weather patterns are influenced by two **winds**: the northeasterly trade winds (the *alisio*) and the easterly or southeasterly wind from the Sahara (the *tiempo del sur*). Two other winds blow very infrequently: a northwesterly wind from the north Atlantic and a southwesterly wind from the tropics. Both carry heavy rains and storms. In winter this usually means snow in the mountains. Only the 'westerlies' carry clouds that sit above Las Cañadas. Luckily these winds are very rare.

The northeasterly trade wind, the *alisio,* which prevails for much of the year, is easily identified by low-lying fluffy clouds — which add so much character to your island photographs. These clouds hover over the north for much of the year. They sit between 600-1500m/2000-5000ft and, above these heights, clear blue skies prevail. Las Cañadas, however, are the only beneficiaries of these beautifully clear days.

The *tiempo del sur,* quite different, brings heat and dust. The temperature rises considerably, and the atmosphere is filled with very fine dust particles. This weather is more frequent in winter than in summer. It seldom lasts more than three or four days. These days are always good for walking (but in summer stay under tree cover!); even if it's a little warm, the sky is cloudless, although a bit hazy.

The only wind that could really spoil your day is the one from the tropics. It *always* brings heavy rains which cover the whole island. This wind is recognisable from its uniform cloud cover. Fortunately it rarely blows.

The winds bring fresh breezes off the sea, making the days very pleasant for walking. And remember, the clouds don't block out the sun altogether; especially on the heights, you will tan (or burn) due to the combination of sun and wind. Don't forget a sunhat! On the other hand, when walking at the higher altitudes, one must always be prepared for the *worst* as well: all seasons can be experienced in one day!

Spanish for walkers

In the countryside, a few words of Spanish can be useful, to greet people and to ask directions.

Here's an almost foolproof way to communicate in Spanish. First, memorise the few short key questions and their possible answers, given below. Then always ask the many questions you can concoct from it **in such a way that you get a 'sí' (yes) or 'no' answer.** *Never* ask an open-ended question such as 'Where is the main road?' Instead, ask the question and then *suggest the most likely answer yourself.* For instance: 'Good day, sir. Please — where is the path to Afur? *Is it straight ahead?'* Now, unless you get a *'si'* response, try: *'Is it to the left?'* If you go through the list of answers to your own question, you will eventually get a *'si'* response — probably with a vigorous nod of the head — and this is more reassuring than relying solely on sign language.

Following are the two most likely situations in which you may have to practice some Spanish. The dots (...) show where you will fill in the name of your destination. Approximate pronunciation of place names is given in the Index, starting on page 133.

▪ Asking the way

The key questions

English	*Spanish*	*pronounced as*
Good day,	Buenos días,	Boo-**eh**-nos **dee**-ahs
sir (madam,	señor (señora,	sen-**yor** (sen-**yo**-rah,
miss).	señorita).	sen-yo-**ree**-tah).
Please —	Por favor —	**Poor** fah-**voor** —
where is	dónde está	**dohn**-day es-**tah**
the road to ...?	la carretera a ...?	la cah-reh-**tay**-rah ah ...?
the path to ...?	la senda de ...?	lah **sen**-dah day ...?
the way to ...?	el camino a ...?	el cah-**mee**-noh ah ...?
the bus stop?	la parada?	lah par-**rah**-dah?
Many thanks.	Muchas gracias.	**Moo**-chas **gra**-thee-as.

Possible answers

is it here?	está aquí?	es-**tah** ah-**kee**?
straight ahead?	todo recto?	**toh**-doh **rec**-toh?
behind?	detrás?	day-**tras**?
to the right?	a la derecha?	ah lah day-**ray**-cha?
to the left?	a la izquierda?	ah lah eeth-kee-**air**-dah?
above?/below?	arriba?/abajo?	ah-**ree**-bah?/ah-**bah**-hoh?

▪ Asking a taxi driver to return for you

English	*Spanish*	*pronounced as*
Please	Por favor	**Poor** fah-**voor**
take us to ...	llévanos a ...	l-**yay**-vah-nos ah ...
and return	y volver	ee vol-**vair**
for us at ...	para nosotros a ...	**pah**-rah nos-**oh**-tros ah ...

(Point out the time when you wish him to return on your watch.)

A country code for walkers and motorists

The experienced rambler is used to following a 'country code' on his walks, but the tourist out for a lark may unwittingly cause damage, harm animals, and even endanger his own life. A code for behaviour is especially important on Tenerife, where the rugged terrain can lead to dangerous mistakes.

- **Only light fires** at picnic areas with fireplaces. Stub out cigarettes with care.
- **Do not frighten animals.** The goats and sheep you may encounter on your walks are not tame. By making loud noises or trying to touch or photograph them, you may cause them to run in fear and be hurt.
- **Walk quietly** through all hamlets and villages, and take care not to provoke the dogs.
- **Leave all gates just as you found them**, whether they are at farms or on the mountainside. Although you may not see any animals, the gates have a purpose: they are used to keep goats or sheep in (or out of) an area. Here again, animals could be endangered by careless behaviour.
- **Protect all wild and cultivated plants.** Don't try to pick wild flowers or uproot saplings. Leave them for other walkers to enjoy. Obviously fruit and other crops are someone's private property and should not be touched.
- **Never walk over cultivated land.**
- **Take all your litter away with you.**
- **DO NOT TAKE RISKS**! This is the most important point of all. Do *not* attempt walks beyond your capacity, and do not wander off the paths described if there is any sign of mist or if it is late in the day. **Do not walk alone**, and *always* tell a responsible person *exactly* where you are going and what time you plan to return. Remember, if you become lost or injure yourself, it may be a long time before you are found. On any but a very short walk near villages, be sure to take a first-aid kit, whistle, torch, extra water and warm clothing — as well as some high-energy food, like chocolate.

Organisation of the walks

The 27 main walks in this book are grouped in four general areas: the Orotava Valley, Las Cañadas, the northwest (including the Teno Peninsula), and the Anaga Peninsula. I hope that the book is set out so that you can plan your walks easily — depending on how far you want to go, your abilities and equipment, and the season.

You might begin by looking at the large fold-out map between pages 16 and 17. Here you can see at a glance the overall terrain, the road network, and the orientation of the walking maps. Quickly flipping through the book, you'll see that there is at least one photograph for every walk, to give you an idea of the landscape.

Having selected one or two potential excursions from the map and the photographs, turn to the relevant walk. At the top of the page you'll find planning information: distance/time, grade, equipment, and how to get there by bus. If the grade and equipment specifications are beyond your scope, don't despair! *There's almost always a short or alternative version of a walk,* and in most cases these are far less demanding of agility and equipment.

When you are on your walk, you will find that the text begins with an introduction to the overall landscape and then quickly turns to a detailed description of the route itself. The large-scale maps (see notes on page 32) have been annotated to show key landmarks. Times are given for reaching certain points in the walk, based on an average walking rate of 3-4km/h and allowing an extra 20 minutes for each 100m/330ft of ascent (fit hikers may complete the walks in half the time). *Do compare your own times with those in the book on a short walk, before you set off on a long hike.* Remember that I've included only *short stops* at viewpoints; allow ample time for photography, picnicking and swimming.

These symbols are used on the walking maps:

principal roads on the touring map (in red)	
minor roads or tracks on the touring map	
track or trail	
path or steps	
water: tank, course, or pipe (in blue)	
main walk (green)	
alternative (green)	
best views	
824	height (m)
forest (green)	
new route	
pylon, wires	
car parking/bus stop	
choza	
P	picnic (pages 10-16)
old route, wrong way	
water gallery	
danger! vertigo!	
church/cemetery or shrine	
habitations, specific building in the text	
rock formations	

1 AGUAMANSA • BENIJOS • C821

Map pages 52-53; nearby photographs pages 51 (bottom), 60 (top)
Distance: 8.5km/5.3mi; 2h10min

Grade: easy; after a level walk, there is a descent of 300m/1000ft.

Equipment: stout shoes, sunhat, cardigan, anorak, raingear, picnic, water

How to get there: 🚌 345 from Puerto to Aguamansa (Timetable 2); journey time 1h
To return: 🚌 345 (Timetable 2) from the C821 to Puerto; journey time 45min; or 🚌 347 (Timetable 10) from Benijos to La Orotava

Alternative walk: Aguamansa — Chanajiga — Palo Blanco: 14km/ 8.7mi; 3h40min; moderate climb of 100m/330ft and descent of 600m/1950ft; equipment as above. Follow the main walk to the remains of Choza A Lugo (1h10min). Here keep straight ahead, now referring to the map on page 77. Ignore all tracks turning uphill or down, until you reach an intersection in 30min, then turn left. Two minutes uphill, bear right. Go right again on reaching a T-junction. At the next intersection, go straight on (there may be a signpost here for Choza Cruz de Luís). At the T-junction before Choza Cruz de Luís (which will be in sight), turn right and, at the Choza, turn right again. Now follow signs to Chanajiga. On reaching the tarred road, follow it left to the car park and picnic area (2h40min). To continue to Palo Blanco (and for return bus information), see notes and map for Walk 13 from the 4h-point (page 79).

This walk is a good starter — it should whet your appetite. The combination of greenery, flowering heather and fragrant pines makes it quite pleasant, and the two water galleries add to the interest.

The Aguamansa bus stop is a wooden shelter on the east side of the road. About 100m/yds beyond it there is a bar/restaurant. When you leave the bus, cross the road and walk uphill about 75m/yds. Then take the wide path on your right; there is a *sendero turístico* (tourist footpath) sign here. Half a minute uphill, when the path forks, bear left. The path takes you to the Piscifactoría de Aguamansa via the rear entrance. When you've looked around, return to the rear entrance to the trout farm and **start the walk**.

Head west along the wide gravel track that enters the pines. Half a minute along, pass below cages holding some indigenous eagles, and soon pass a drinking fountain below the track. Two minutes later, after rounding a bend, climb stone steps to your left (there may be a sign for La Caldera here). About 30m/yds up, you may spot a table and benches to the left, but bear right on a narrow earthen path through heather. Breaks in the vegetation permit open views down to Aguamansa.

About 10 minutes later (**15min**) meet a fairly wide gravel track and turn right. (Ignore the track on the right half a minute ahead.) Weather permitting, the volcanic cone of El Teide will be in full view, peeping over the western wall of the Orotava Valley. From this vantage point, however, it's difficult to believe that this is Spain's highest mountain (3718m/12,195ft)!

On coming to a fork (**30min**) bear right downhill to the Galería La Fortuita, one of the island's many water sources. From these *galerías* (tunnels), water is piped to all parts of the island. The water is tapped from underground 'reservoirs', where there is a continuous supply of water resulting from condensation (the Canary pine plays a particularly important role: see notes on page 45). Tenerife relies very heavily on these water sources, because there are no natural wells and few streams with a permanent flow of water.

After returning to the main track, ignore the fork to the right at **45min**. Ten minutes later you enter a narrow gulley and cross an old stone bridge above a dry river bed with huge boulders. Two minutes round the bend, a steep gravel track branches off at a right angle: ignore it. At this point, a second *galería* appears — Pino Soler. Pines announce the beginning of the forest.

Meet a junction at about **1h** (where there *may* still be a sign for Choza Antonio Lugo). Turn right downhill and, two minutes later, you'll meet a fork: don't turn right; continue straight ahead. The remains of Choza Antonio Lugo can be seen above the track five minutes later (**1h10min**). Here you turn right for Benijos *(but for the Alternative walk, continue straight ahead).*

You start out for Benijos on a disused track. Five minutes downhill, at an intersection, continue straight down on another track. At **1h20min** this track branches off left to a farm: go right, down a grassy trail that follows the edge of the forest. At the next fork, keep straight ahead past a large, lone pine; don't turn right. Puerto soon comes into view. The trail drops suddenly to rejoin the gravel track you turned off a little earlier. Continue down to the right. The dogs will have picked up your scent by now and let those further downhill know you're on your way. They'll all bark, and some may run up to stone-throwing distance, but that's about all the energy they'll summon up. The track eventually becomes a concrete lane and leads to the TF2125 near Benijos (**1h45min**). You *can* catch a bus here (to La Orotava), but they are infrequent. Bear right to the C821 (**2h10min**), where the bus stop is almost facing you.

2 AGUAMANSA • LA CALDERA • CHOZA CHIMOCHE • PEDRO GIL • AGUAMANSA

Map pages 52-53; photographs pages 49 (top), 60 (bottom)

Distance: 8km/5mi; 3h40min

Grade: easy-moderate climb/descent of 400m/1300ft; the descent from Pedro Gil is steep.

Equipment: stout shoes, sunhat, cardigan, anorak, raingear, picnic, water

How to get there: 🚌 345 from Puerto to Aguamansa (Timetable 2); journey time 1h; alight at the *trout farm (piscifactoría).*
To return: 🚌 345 from Aguamansa trout farm to Puerto (as above)

Short walk: Aguamansa — La Caldera — Aguamansa: 3km/2mi; just over 1h; easy. Follow the main walk to the crater, circle it, and return the same way. Why not combine this with part of Walk 1 — perhaps going to Galería La Fortuita and return?

Here's a short walk with plenty of variety — patches of forest, ravines, high and naked escarpments, shady moss-green paths, and idyllic viewing points.

Start out at the trout farm. From the main entrance, cross the road and head uphill for some 30m/yds, to where a narrow gravel track turns off right into pines and heather. Follow the wide earthen path forking right, just at the start of this track. It takes you directly behind the bus shelter. Pines and dense heather flank the way. Ignore a branch-off to the right a few minutes uphill. Five minutes up, cross over a forestry track; then ignore another small path to the right a few minutes later. In **25min** come to a fairly wide gravel track and turn right. Behind you is the impressive mountain range enclosing the eastern side of the Orotava Valley. On reaching the tarred road that circles La Caldera, bear right; through the trees, you will see the crater *(la caldera)* below you on your left. There's a pleasant bar/restaurant ahead and beyond it a large parking area and bus stop.

Continue by circling the crater on the road. Ignore a first track off to the right, but bear right on the next track (signposted 'Pasada Las Bestias, Pedro Gil/Chimoche'). *For the Short walk remain on the tarred road here.* Follow this gravel track through slender pines. At under **1h25min** turn right on the main track, where an earthen track (our return route) continues straight on. A small gorge lies below. Beyond an enormous gravel deposit, you

Choza Chimoche

pass Galería Chimoche, a very important water source (see notes page 40). Behind the two buildings, hidden in the rocky-faced embankment, is the *galería* ('water gallery' or tunnel). The **2h**-mark brings you into a relatively clear area and the shelter Choza Chimoche (Picnic 2; see bottom photograph page 60). Continue up the track at the left of the shelter for a few minutes, to an even lovelier picnic spot by the mouth of a ravine. This is the wildest section of the hike.

From the ravine re-trace your steps for 30 minutes and head back to more garden-like surroundings. Your turn-off is the T-junction about 10 minutes below the *galería*. The track to the left is the route you climbed from La Caldera; you now head right for Pedro Gil on a narrow earthen track which skirts the ravine below. Ten minutes from the turn-off (**2h40min**) come to a small flat area called Pedro Gil. (The track ends just around the bend.)

From Pedro Gil you descend to the left on a path marked by a cairn. A minute down, pass a small shrine on the right. The **2h55min**-point is marked by three wooden crosses on the Camino de las Crucitas (Path of the Little Crosses). From this serene spot, you can see a forestry track below on your right: it goes to Choza El Topo and Choza Almadi (Walk 4). You soon meet it.

When you join this track, go straight ahead 30m/yds, to a tree bearing two yellow circles and a *sendero turístico* sign. Don't turn right along the track. Take the path behind the tree; a small cairn marks it. The path is darkened by tall heather, leafy trees, and the occasional pine. It's a cool, green return. The trees here wear 'beards' of moss and lichen (photograph page 58).

Having crossed a track, you reach the base of Galería La Puente at **3h15min**. From here continue on the only track leaving this water source; head right. On your way, do stop for a minute to look behind you. Los Organos (the Organ Pipes; photograph page 60, top) are in full view. A few minutes along, you pass a track forking off to the right. Just beyond it, you'll see your return path, also on the right: it's the path you ascended from Aguamansa. Small cairns clearly mark the departure point. Two minutes downhill the path collides with a magnificent old pine that must be about 5m/15ft in circumference at the base of its trunk. Ignore all the narrow side-paths, and in five minutes you will reach the main road and your bus stop (**3h40min**).

3 AGUAMANSA • PINOLERIS • LA FLORIDA

Map pages 52-53; photographs pages 49 (bottom), 51 (bottom)

Distance: 4.5km/2.8mi; 1h30min

Grade: moderate descent of 550m/1800ft. *Although the route is now all tarred, this is a very popular walk.*

Equipment: stout shoes, sunhat, cardigan, anorak, raingear, picnic, water

How to get there: 🚌 345 from Puerto to Aguamansa (Timetable 2); journey time 1h

To return: 🚌 346 from La Florida to La Orotava (not in the timetables; departs hourly at 45min past the hour); journey time 10min; *change to* 🚌 350 (Timetable 3); journey time 30min

Alternative walk: Aguamansa — Choza Chimoche — La Florida: 13km/8mi; 5h20min; moderate climb of 400m/1300ft and descent of 900m/2950ft; equipment and access as above. Do Walk 2, then descend to Aguamansa and continue with this walk.

Here's a perfect rural setting of peaceful farmlands rolling out of valleys. Bright-blooming flower beds enliven country cottages, wild fields are grazed under the watchful eyes of shepherds, ageing chestnuts stand guard over the declining slopes, and neat stone walls hide the season's produce. With luck, the shielding eastern arm of the Orotava Valley will discard its veil of mist, revealing fine views of its pine-clad slopes.

Start out at the Aguamansa bus shelter: head downhill into the village (signposted). Then take the first right turn (signposted to Mamio, Pinoleris and La Florida). From here on you follow the country road shown on page 51 (bottom). Colour and greenery flow out of the landscape all the way. Hedges of white-flowering chimney broom (*escobón*) border the fields. Spot a reservoir over to the left, and in **20min** meet a junction: turn left. A well-cared-for shrine, on a bend, is passed a few minutes later. Here, keep straight on (Walk 5 and Short walk 4 come in here via the farm track on the right). Ignore the fork to the right two minutes along. Enjoy an uninterrupted view of Puerto before descending quite suddenly; then bear sharp right at a fork.

The road curves back sharply left and descends to a T-junction (**50min**). Bear left through Pinoleris. Two minutes down, by a church, the road swings left; go right here, straight downhill, on another road. At a T-junction in La Florida Alta (**1h05min**), keep left downhill. Ignore a small turn-off left in a few minutes but, at the next T-junction, continue downhill to the left. Beyond the school, you reach the bus stop (**1h30min**). Or walk on to the C821, 15 minutes to your left, to catch one of the frequent buses to Puerto.

4 LA CALDERA • CHOZA EL TOPO • CHOZA ALMADI • PINO ALTO • LA FLORIDA

Map pages 52-53; photographs pages 49 (top) 50, 51 (top), 58, 60 (top)

Distance: 16.5km/10.2mi; 6h

Grade: easy-moderate climb of 350m/1150ft beyond Choza El Topo, followed by a strenuous descent of 1000m/3300ft beyond Choza Almadi. This descent sometimes crosses loose gravel and *can be very dangerous in wet conditions.* Pay particular attention to the weather. Even if it looks only *slightly* bad, don't risk this walk. There are only two shelters between La Caldera and Pino Alto, and temperatures can drop very suddenly on these heights (1200m/4000ft and above).

Equipment: walking boots, sunhat, warm cardigan, anorak, raingear, whistle, picnic, water

How to get there: 🚌 345 from Puerto to La Caldera (Timetable 2); journey time 1h05min
To return: 🚌 346 from La Florida to La Orotava (not in the timetables; departs hourly at 45min past the hour); journey time 10min; *change to* 🚌 350 (Timetable 3); journey time 30min

Short walk: La Caldera — Choza El Topo — Choza Perez Ventoso — Aguamansa: 6km/3.7mi; 2h05min; easy, level walking to Choza El Topo, followed by a steep descent of 200m/650ft to Choza Perez Ventoso. Stout shoes or walking boots, sunhat, cardigan, picnic, water. Follow the main walk for 1h; then use the notes for Walk 5 from the 4h30min-point (page 50).

This walk requires a little energy, as you'll head up into cloud territory at about 1450m/4750ft. But wherever you pull up to rest, a panorama will unfold around you. For most of the way, your views sweep along the whole Orotava Valley, from El Teide down to the ocean, and over to the western tip of the island. Beautiful grand old pines cling to the steep slopes. Poised upright with their beckoning branches, they remind one of Balinese dancers in a moment of pause. The rocky ravine floors that cut into the mountainside have long since dried up and wait for the sharp winter downpours to briefly cleanse them.

The bar at La Caldera, near where you leave the bus, is **the starting point** for this walk. Walk past the bar and then fork left on the gravel forestry track signposted to Los Organos, the rock formation shown in the top photograph on page 60. And indeed, a small eroded section of this range looks very much like a row of organ pipes *(organos).* This track through heather and pines is easy to follow, and there are no major turn-offs. Not far along, you cross a bridge which straddles the end of a narrow ravine, the Barranco de Pedro Gil.

About **10min** along, various signs appear, including one for Choza El Topo. Walks 5 and 6 head south here, to Pedro Gil; keep to the main track. In the sweeping U-shaped curve of the track, you'll notice a pine-covered slope. These tall and gracious trees look almost ornamental, with long wisps of pale green lichen hanging from their branches (see photograph page 58). There are more such corners further on. The highest farms in the valley, nestled in against the walls of the escarpment, lie a little below the track. The fields up here are not cultivated and seem to have reverted to grass. Groves of chestnuts are loosely scattered below the route. Lower down, orchards can be seen through the pines. An old bridge, crossing a dry river bed, marks the **35min**-point in the walk. Five minutes later, ignore a turn-off to the left.

Choza El Topo is reached **1h** from La Caldera. A table and bench await the tired and hungry. This shelter is another good viewing spot for the Orotava Valley. Keep straight on beyond this shelter *(but for the Short walk, bear left on the path behind the choza)*. Within the next twenty minutes, the real ascent begins. Carved into the mountainside, the track now zigzags lazily up towards Choza Almadi. It's a steady climb. There's a possibility that you'll be swallowed up by clouds or mist as you approach the summit of the track, at 1450m/4750ft. Your way curves back into an inner valley in the range, and then begins to descend out into the Orotava Valley again, with good views of the Los Organos mass of dissected rock. A little further along, the coastline unrolls.

Notice the dampness in the air. On cloudy days, all the plants are saturated with dew, giving rise to an interesting phenomenon: the majestic Canary pine plays a very important ecological role. The

Canary pine (Pinus canariensis)

prevailing northerly winds carry clouds to the northern slopes, and create an atmosphere which causes condensation. The drippings from this moisture were measured over the period of a year and yield an incredible 2000 litres per square metre! This may not mean much to you — until I tell you that a reasonable rainfall for a year gives about 500 litres per square metre! This is the reason for the continuous planting of trees in bare or denuded areas of the forest: to feed the underground reservoirs described on page 40.

As you approach Choza Almadi (**3h**) varying shades of browns from the ploughed plots far below and green from sprouting plants will delight you. Come to an intersection. The *choza* sits below the track. Take a break here, before beginning the descent. Then turn left immediately and head straight downhill below the shelter. This descent (marked by occasional *sendero turístico* signs) is so steep that you'll find yourself almost leaning backwards! Some grand old trees tower overhead.

Fifteen minutes below Choza Almadi, your track joins another, fainter track, and continues downhill. (If you are ever in doubt, just continue straight down!) Under 10 minutes further down, meet another track on a wide bend. A minute round the bend, take the fork off to the left. Some five minutes further on, come to Cruz de las Lajitas (**3h30min**), the viewpoint shown on page 50. The place has some religious significance and (when it hasn't fallen over) a 10m/30ft-high white metal cross stands out clearly here, on the edge of the ridge. There is also a small white shrine to the left, buried in flowers. Perhaps these are meant to safeguard those descending the mountain. While the entire walk has offered a series of wonderful subjects for the camera, I think that from here you have the most complete view of the Orotava Valley.

A second clearing is reached just a little further on: take the earthen track to the left, going straight downhill. Five minutes downhill, when this track forks (at the 1100m contour on the map), go left again. Meet another track under 10 minutes later and again bear left. A couple of minutes along (at the 1000m contour), bear right at the fork. (This is a new route, marked with arrows on the map. The trail shown in green on the map is marked with an X at this point: it is very overgrown, and there is no signposting. If you have a good sense of direction and don't mind following overgrown paths and trails, you may prefer to follow the route shown in green on the map. It *is* still viable and would save you about 2.5km walking on the forestry track. You would come out at the 5h-point in the text, where you bear left on the road.)

Somewhat over 10 minutes later, watch for a path forking off left. (There may be a signpost 'TM Santa Ursula' about 100m/yds *before* this path.) The path is just beyond a lone pine and also continues uphill on the other side of the track. Descend this path. Under 10 minutes downhill, come to a T-juntion, where a track cuts in front of you. Bear left and, five minutes later, meet the main track again. Keep left here and now follow this main track all the way. Eventually it becomes tarred.

Remain on this road, keeping left at the junction 10 minutes along. At **5h** you pass a roadside shrine. Two minutes later, on the right (just beyond a house with a tall lone palm tree in its garden), you may be able to pick up the short-cut paths shown on the map to descend to Pino Alto but, if they are too overgrown, you will have to stay on the road.

Pino Alto appears, now only minutes away. Perched above the rest of the valley, this typical Canarian village has superb views. You reach a T-junction where there is a fine viewpoint — an ideal place to get your breath back and absorb your surroundings. Then turn left. As you've not got far to go now, you can just meander down the narrow shady street. Heads will pop out of dark doorways, as they catch the echo of your passing footsteps. The escarpment wall rises up protectively behind the village and, below, vineyards (which produce a white wine) cover most of the land.

Following a steep descent and then a slight climb, you'll reach a T-junction which marks the beginning of La Florida at **6h**. The bus stop is here at the T-junction. Two bars are downhill on the left-hand side of the road. The C821 (where you can catch more frequent buses) is 15 minutes to the right.

5 LA CALDERA • PEDRO GIL • CHOZA EL TOPO • AGUAMANSA

Map pages 52-53; photographs pages 49 (top), 51 (bottom), 60 (top)

Distance: 12.5km/7.8mi; 5h35min

Grade: fairly strenuous climb of 400m/1300ft and descent of 500m/1650ft. *Not recommended for inexperienced walkers* because of the **danger of vertigo** beyond Pedro Gil (although there is a handrail along many of the vertiginous places).

Equipment: stout shoes or walking boots, sunhat, warm cardigan, anorak, raingear, picnic, water

How to get there: 🚌 345 from Puerto to La Caldera (Timetable 2); journey time 1h05min
To return: 🚌 345 from Aguamansa to Puerto (Timetable 2); journey time 1h

Shorter walk: La Caldera — spectacular chasm — La Caldera: 9km/5.6mi; 4h15min; grade and equipment as above; **danger of vertigo.** Follow the main walk for 2h15min, then return the same way for 🚌 345.

Have you ever wondered what lies *above* Los Organos? This walk takes you up into cloud-catching peaks. Between these fractured pinnacles lie chasms of exuberant vegetation.

Start out by walking past the bar at La Caldera (Picnic 5a). Take the first turn on your left, the wide gravel track shown in the photograph at the top of page 60. In **10min** you come to signs for 'Pedro Gil/Chimoche' and 'Camino a Candelaria': take the wide earthen path behind a cairn. (Walk 4 continues along the track here.) The three little crosses you pass give this path its name: Camino de Las Crucitas (Way of the Crosses). A shrine and eucalyptus trees mark the end of this path: Pedro Gil, a small, flat area reached in **35min.**

Now cross a track and follow the path (marked with hiking peg no 4) straight ahead up the hillside. The way divides here and there, braiding itself up the slope. The side-on view of Los Organos and the eastern escarpment are quite impressive. It's hard to believe that the route winds up into those walls!

At just over **55min**, a path branches off right; keep left. A few minutes later (**1h**), turn left at a major junction, marked by hiking peg no 5. (Walk 6 turns right here, to make for La Crucita.) *Stretches of the ongoing path are alarmingly vertiginous for about the next fifty minutes.* Not far around the slope, you'll notice hundreds of the small rosette plants shown here (*Greenovia aurea*) on

Greenovia aurea

Pink-flowering Cistus flanks the route between Pedro Gil and the Los Organos turn-off; this setting is typical of Walks 2, 4, 5, 6 and 7.

the rock face. Grey-green velvet-leafed bushes (*Sideritis* or 'Canarian edelweiss') will also catch your eye.

Water, trickling down a vertical rock face (a seasonal flow), marks the **1h15min**-point in the walk. You leave the Chimoche side of the slope and climb above Los Organos. Pass a viewing point with a handrail on a rocky promontory in **2h**, and soon you enter a plunging gorge, surrounded by precipitous sharp peaks. Handrails here help to allay feelings of vertigo. At about **2h15min** the end of the gorge is reached. *The Shorter walk turns back here.*

On clear days you will enjoy a fine view of Aguamansa's trout farm at just over **2h20min**. Beyond this viewpoint the path progresses eastwards, zigzagging up

Walk 3: between Pinoleris and La Florida; the vineyard below the thatched hut is interplanted with cabbages.

The Orotava Valley from Cruz de las Lajitas (Walk 4)

and down across what seems inaccessible terrain. At about **2h30min** you swing into an enormous valley deep in the escarpment (where you may have to scramble over a rock-slide). On leaving it, soon find yourself in a forest of gigantic pines.

Several minutes into the wood, ***watch carefully for your turn-off on the left.*** This should be marked by hiking peg no 11 and an arrow; however the hiking pegs are not always in place. This is a very important turn-off which you ***must not miss,*** because the path continuing to the right becomes *impassable* after half an hour, and *you are in potentially dangerous terrain.* The path you want heads down towards a large rocky 'hump'; you descend a ramp made of rocks just before reaching the 'hump'. Once below the rocks, look for the largest pine ahead (slightly to the left). Behind this giant tree the path becomes clearer and eventually widens out into a faint forestry track.

On joining a track coming from the right (**3h20min**), keep left. Under an hour downhill, meet a T-junction and turn right. Five minutes later, ignore a fork to the right. Soon the Choza Almadi track (Walk 4) cuts across in front of you, and you are opposite Choza El Topo (**4h30min**; Picnic 4). Beyond this shelter, your hike will become more countrified.

Descend the path on the right, behind the shelter. It widens to a track. Under 10 minutes down, fork right on a path (the track continues down to your left). You will have clear views of the entire valley and the sea. In another 10 minutes, at an intersection, bear left on the

At Choza Almadi (Walk 4)

second track. It descends very steeply to Choza Perez Ventoso (**5h**; Picnic 5b). *Bear* right here (don't turn right immediately): follow a farm track towards a concrete shed. Stone walls lead you past neatly-cultivated fields and to a picturesque junction (**5h05min**): a shrine sits comfortably in a stone wall on the left. Cacti, geraniums and chrysanthemums edge the sides of the road. A quaint little house backs onto all of this. (Walk 3 descends to Pinoleris opposite the shrine.)

Turn left along the road shown below. Minutes later bear right at a fork. At the T-junction in Aguamansa (**5h30min**) turn left for a short stiff climb to the C821 and your bus stop (**5h35min**). Rooftops weighed down with vividly-coloured hanging plants are the last memories of this walk through incredibly varied landscapes.

Pico del Teide from Aguamansa (Walks 3, 5; Picnic 5b; Car tour 1)

Walks 1-5; also 6, 7

Walk 1 starts at the trout farm and goes west to Benijos and the C821.
Walk 2 starts at the trout farm, circles La Caldera and climbs to Choza Chimoche, returning to Aguamansa by a different route.
Walk 3 starts at the Aguamansa bus stop and heads north to La Florida.
Walk 4 starts at La Caldera, follows a track below Los Organos and then climbs to Choza Almadi before descending to La Florida.
Walk 5 starts at La Caldera, follows a path above Los Organos and descends to Aguamansa via Choza Perez Ventoso.

The beginning of Walk 6 and the end of Walk 7 are also shown:
Walk 6 follows the route of Walk 5 for 40min; at this point Walk 5 forks left and Walk 6 forks right, climbing above the Choza Chimoche path, before heading east to La Crucita.
Walk 7 descends to Choza Chimoche, then follows Walk 2 (in reverse) to La Caldera.

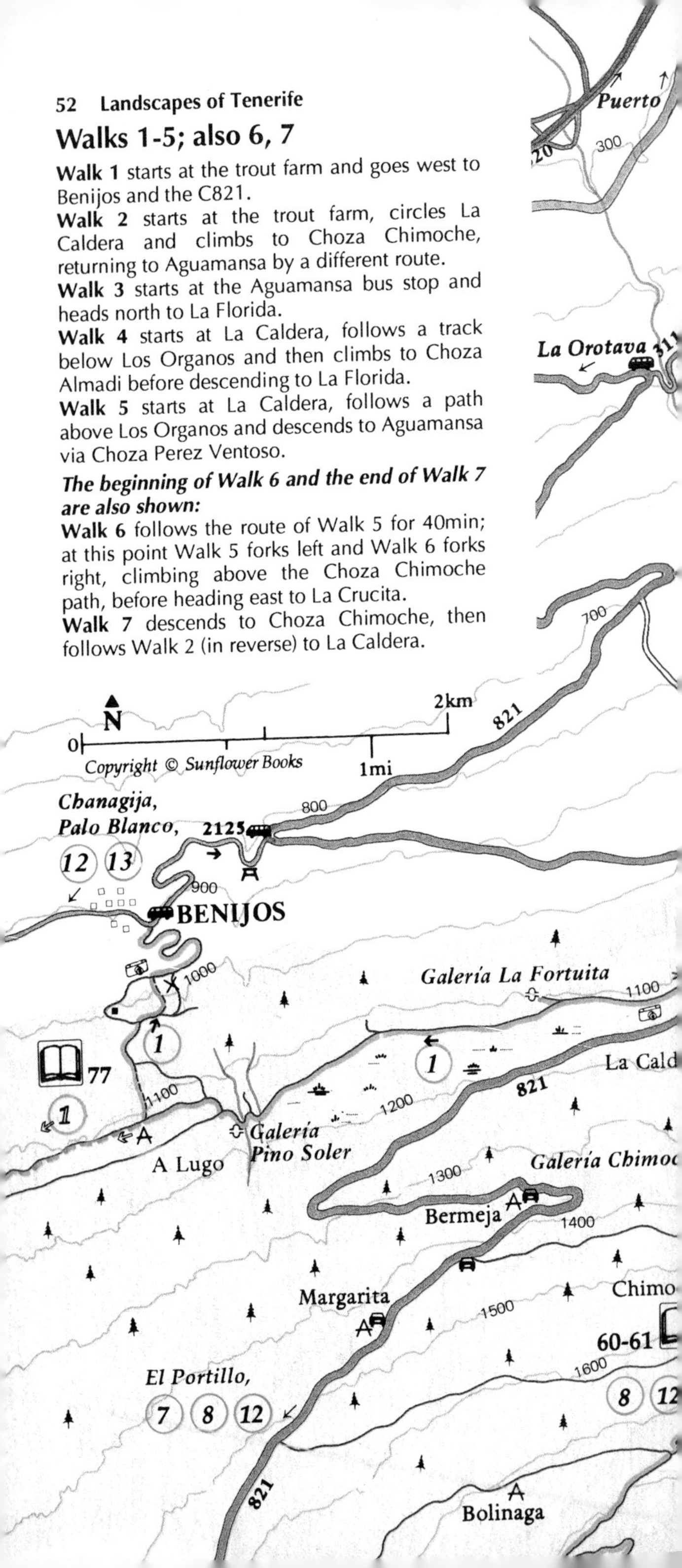

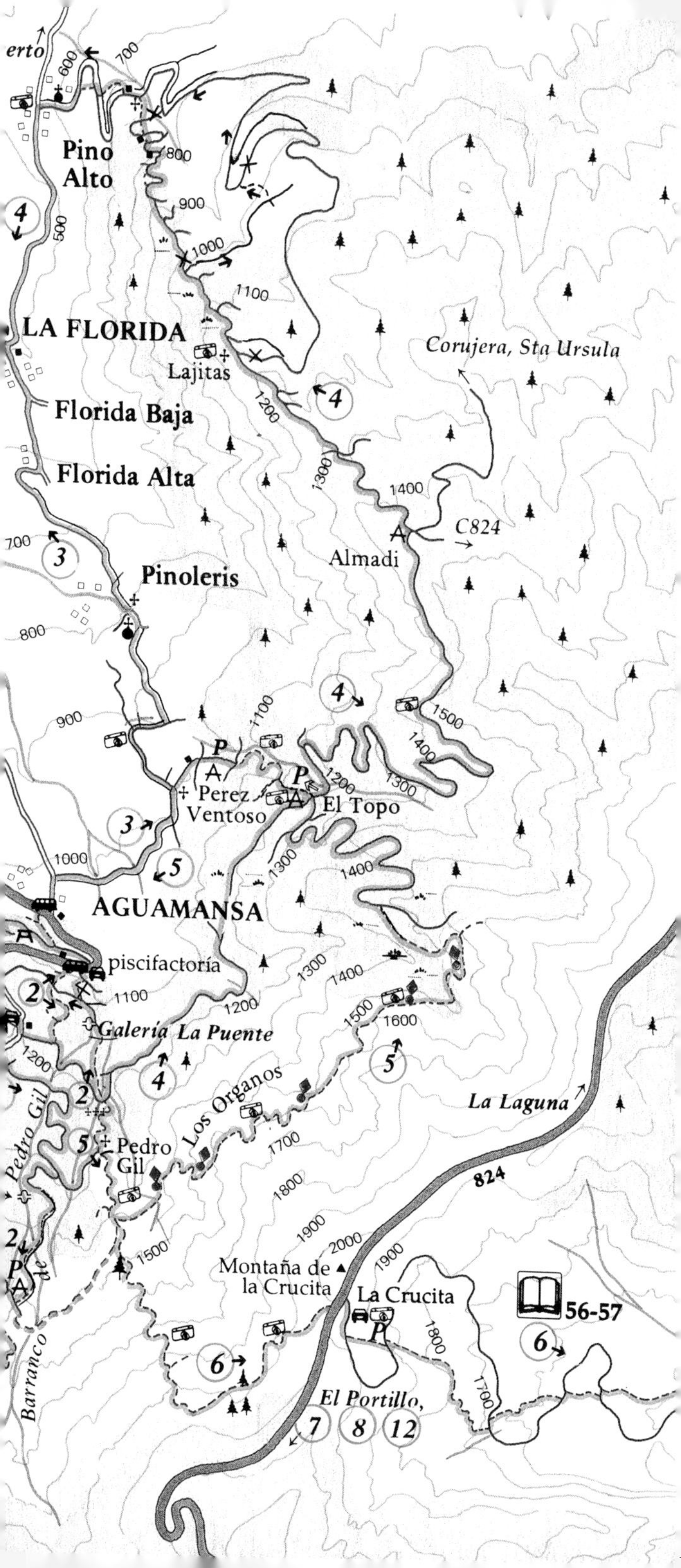

erto
Pino Alto
LA FLORIDA
Lajitas
Florida Baja
Florida Alta
Corujera, Sta Ursula
Almadi
C824
Pinoleris
Perez Ventoso
El Topo
AGUAMANSA
piscifactoría
Galería La Puente
Los Organos
Pedro Gil
Barranco de Pedro Gil
La Laguna
824
Montaña de la Crucita
La Crucita
56-57
El Portillo,

6 THE CANDELARIA TRAIL: LA CALDERA • LA CRUCITA • ARAFO

Use the map on pages 52-53 as far as La Crucita and the map on pages 56-57 from La Crucita to Arafo. See also photographs page 49 (top), 60 (top)

Distance: 12.5km/7.8mi; 6h

Grade: very strenuous, with a steep climb (800m/2600ft) and steep gravelly descent (1500m/4950ft)

Equipment: walking boots, sunhat, warm cardigan, anorak, raingear, long trousers, whistle, picnic, water

How to get there: 🚌 345 from Puerto to La Caldera (Timetable 2); journey time 1h05min
To return: 🚌 121 from Arafo to Santa Cruz (not in the timetables): departs Arafo at 45min past the hour until 19.45 (hourly Mon-Fri; every *second* hour Sat, Sun, holidays); journey time 50min; *change to* 🚌 102 to Puerto (Timetable 1); journey time 1h

Short walk: La Caldera — Pedro Gil — Choza Chimoche — La Caldera: 5.5km/3.5mi; 2h25min; easy-moderate climb/descent of 300m/1000ft; equipment as above, but stout shoes will suffice. Referring to the map on pages 52-53, follow the main walk to the junction met at 1h. Just uphill from the junction, below the large pine, bear right on a path. The path ends at the Barranco de Pedro Gil (1h20min). From here follow the forestry track for a couple of minutes, down to Choza Chimoche. To return to La Caldera, pick up Walk 7 at the 5h20min-point (page 60).

This hike follows an old pilgrims' way known as the Candelaria Trail. It originally began at La Orotava. It climbs the steep escarpment of the central massif and then twists endlessly down to the sea at Candelaria. Today, the land between Arafo and Candelaria is so built-up that the few pilgrims who still make the journey leave the trail at your destination, Arafo. The Virgin of Candelaria is Tenerife's patron saint, whose Assumption is celebrated each year on August 14-15th. This long, but gratifying walk offers superb panoramas, encompassing corners of immense beauty.

Start out by following Walk 5 for **1h**, to hiking peg No 5. Here Walk 5 bears left: turn *right.* Barely a minute up from the hiking peg, the main path veers off round the right-hand side of the ridge. You do *not!* At this point you are just below a large pine: continue up the ridge, to the left of the pine. *(The path to the right leads to Chimoche and is the Short walk route.)*

Montaña de las Arenas, the setting for Walk 6, from the main road at La Crucita (Picnic 6, Car tour 5)

As the climb steepens, more of the valley becomes visible through the sparse pine growth. Half an hour from the last turn-off, on a bend, you look over into a strip of bare *barranco* that emanates a soft mixture of pinks, mauves, browns and greys. Seconds up, your path briefly runs alongside a thin, vertical wall of serrated rock. The vegetation undergoes a change here: small bushes of Canarian edelweiss (*Sideritis*) turn white as their velvety leaves catch the sun, and scraggy chimney broom (*escobón*) and *retama* take control of the slope. The path is so colourful that it's easy to forget the wider landscapes on view.

All the way up, the vast view focuses on the productive greens of La Orotava. At **2h15min** you'll find yourself sheltered between a low wall of rock and a clump of pines. A faded arrow on the wall points you through a gap. From here, you can see your path heading across the escarpment. Another patch of writing on rocks, and a white arrow pointing left, will be your next landmark. The path climbs steeply through rocks and over stones. A good look-out point, over the wall fencing off the ridge, comes up at **2h40min**, and soon the main road to La Laguna (C824) is in view up ahead.

By **3h** you reach La Crucita (Picnic 6) at an altitude of 1980m/6500ft. From here on it's down, down! So get out your anchor! Head down the southern escarpment, cross the road and, 50m/yds downhill on the right, turn onto a forestry track. The isolated valley you are about to enter lies far below. The entrance to the valley is

blocked by an enormous naked black mound, Las Arenas. You have the stupendous view shown on pages 54-55: dark, pine-sprinkled slopes drop down to a coastal plain tessellated in faded browns and greens. The sea stretches out into the distance.

Three minutes down the track (see map below), your path takes off on the left and slithers its way down the stark slope. Your descent will be at a snail's pace — it's all loose gravel and the slope looks almost vertical. Within minutes, you'll cross the track. Turn left: your continuation is 10m/yds downhill, on the right. Soon head back into pines, under which *codéso* and broom shelter. Rejoin the track but, 20m/yds downhill, find the path on your left, on a bend. It squiggles through the trees, no longer as clear as it was. But the unhappy sight of discarded litter tells you you're more or less on course. Keep the shallow ravine on your left within sight, and you're sure to be okay.

Recross the track once more, and again find your path slightly below and to the left. It soon fades out. Descend to the left of a slight crease in the slope. At the next track crossing, find your ongoing path again a few metres downhill and on the left. A large boulder with a few rocks on it marks the entry point. A minute down finds you in a shallow *barranco:* descend this for a couple of minutes and then swing out of the ravine and onto the crest. Keep along the left-hand side of the crest as you continue.

Smooth black sand soon comes underfoot. The outline of a rounded volcanic hill, Las Arenas, completely disrupts the landscape as it appears through the trees. You come face-to-face with this bulging black monster at **4h15min**. It obliterates everything. The track is not far below; shortly, you rejoin it. Follow it down for about a minute; then, on the next bend, cut off right across the sand. On meeting the track again, leave it after two

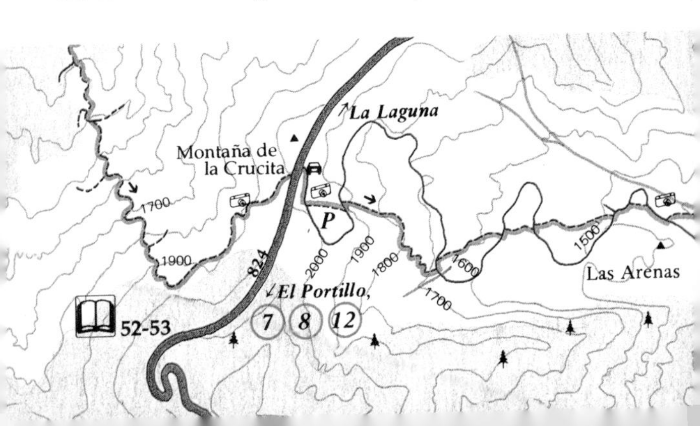

minutes: take the small path just past a metal gate (and marked by an orange dot on a stone) and keep alongside the ravine. (The track heads slightly away from the ravine, to the right, at this point.) Gran Canaria is on the horizon. Arafo, your destination, is far below, and the immediate landscape reveals an intriguing beauty: chestnut trees are the sole survivors in these black sands. Bent and crippled, these 'triffid' creatures have never managed to raise their backs. It's a unique sight.

When next you meet the track on a bend (**4h20min**) turn right on it. In ten minutes you reach a simple stone refuge that the pilgrims visit. To return to the path, head to the bend in the track just below the refuge and take the small path down to your left; it returns you to the main path. You leave the desert for scrub and bushes.

Scrubland is eventually replaced by a Canary pine forest, and you pass some proud old specimens. The way splinters and rejoins. Ignore the faint path forking left: keep straight downhill. Shortly your way swings across the hillside and, in under five minutes, you strike off right on a path. Cross an old *canal* a minute down. Five minutes past the *canal*, you come to the edge of the forest, where small paths lead left and right: continue straight on between crumbled walls, with overgrown plots on your right. A few minutes down, you're accompanied part way by another small *canal*; another joins a few minutes later, and brings you into wine country. Then your path joins a track (**5h20min**).

From now on, head *straight down*, whether by path or track or road, to arrive at Arafo (**5h45min**). Here meet a narrow tarred road: turn right. Pass between the houses and turn left at the junction. Walk past a tiny bubbling fountain, benches, and flower troughs splashing out colour. Take the first right and come to the main square (**6h**), where you pick up your bus.

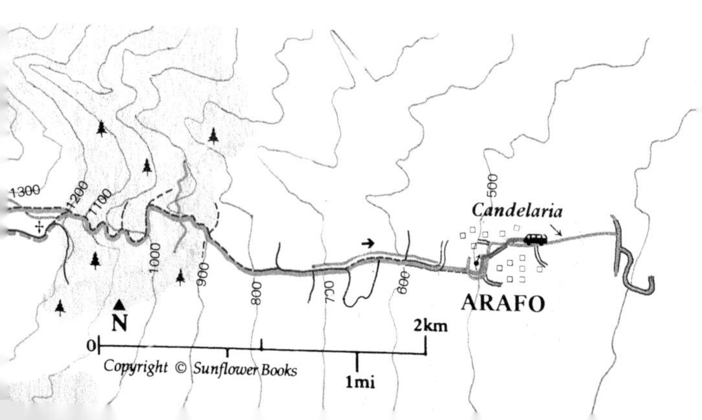

7 EL PORTILLO • CORRAL DEL NIÑO • CHOZA CHIMOCHE • LA CALDERA

Distance: 17km/10.5mi; 6h20min

Grade: moderate, with an ascent of 250m/820ft at the start and a fairly steep descent of 1000m/3300ft

Equipment: stout shoes, sunhat, warm cardigan, anorak, raingear, picnic, water

How to get there: 🚌 348 from Puerto to El Portillo (Timetable 5); journey time 1h20min
To return: 🚌 345 from La Caldera to Puerto (Timetable 2); journey time 1h05min

Short walk: El Portillo — Corral del Niño — El Portillo: 9km/5.5mi; 3h30min; easy ascent and descent of 250m/820ft *on a road;* equipment as above. 🚌 348 (as above) to go and return.

A rolling landscape of perfectly rounded volcanic mounds, mellow, glistening slopes, and the occasional chirp of calling birds sets this walk apart from the others. Almost two hours along a tarred road does not sound a very appealing beginning to a walk. But the C824 is not a busy road, except on weekends. The striking natural beauty of the landscape is so absorbing that the little traffic encountered passes unnoticed.

Start out in front of El Portillo's restaurant: head east on the La Laguna road (C824). Montaña Alta will be your first significant landmark, on your left. You'll pass

Lichen-festooned pines between Choza El Topo and Choza Almadi (Walk 4) — a setting typical of many island walks

El Teide from Cruz de Fregel (Walk 12; near Walk 7, Picnic 12b and Car tours 1 and 5)

the small gravel track to its *choza* (Picnic 7a) in about **15min.** Along the roadside, the white and yellow blooms of *margarita del Teide, retama* and Canary flaxweed prove their worth in springtime. The road climbs some 250m/820ft to Corral del Niño. Being just outside the perimeter of the crater, it is not exactly like the landscape of Las Cañadas (Walk 8) — it lacks the aggressive sharpness. There's a smooth, flowing undulation here. As you progress, El Teide becomes complete behind you, and there are wide-ranging views of the Orotava Valley on cloudless days.

In under **2h**, just before the 'Corral del Niño' sign (*where the Short walk turns back*), you turn off left on a wide track. It takes you into a rolling sea of colours. The sun catches all the hidden tones as you follow the contours. You're crossing a giant palette, as you head down for the pines far below. Pebble-sized scoria (see photograph page 64) covers much of the land, and volcanic mounds rise like giant anthills.

In **3h** arrive at Choza J Ruiz de Izaña. From here follow the path opposite the shelter, across the forestry track. Rejoin the track in two minutes and turn left. Barely one minute along (some 75m/yds), bear right on another path (marked by a cairn), hedged in by *retama. Sendero turístico* signs pop up along the way. Montaña de Limón, a small volcanic mound with burgundy-red slopes soon comes into view on your right.

At **3h20min** you're approaching the forest: it begins rather shyly, with small scattered pines. The path zig-

Los Organos (the 'Organ Pipes') rise near La Caldera. This photograph was taken from the forestry track followed in Walks 4, 5 and 6.

The track between Choza J Ruiz de Izaña and Choza Chimoche (Walk 7; near Walk 2 and Picnic 2).

zags symmetrically down to the track (**3h40min**): turn right. You'll see plants with twigs like bottle-brushes, called *codéso.* During the winter, they're just a pleasing green, but in spring they enliven the landscape with their brilliant yellow blossoms. Some 20 minutes downhill, meet a T-junction and turn right.

At **4h30min**, you leave the track: take the path on the right, marked by a small pile of rocks on the right and a cairn signed 'Cuevas de Limón' on the left. (The track continues left to Choza Bolinaga and the C821, with a good viewpoint seven minutes downhill.) Your path, to Choza Chimoche, now steepens considerably. Layers of soft pine needles cover the loose stones. Cross another forestry track at **4h50min**, to find the continuing path about 3m/yds along on your right. A cairn marks it. Descend steeply, edging round a beautiful wide ravine with a forested floor. Half an hour of steep zigzagging brings you to Choza Chimoche (**5h20min**) and onto another track.

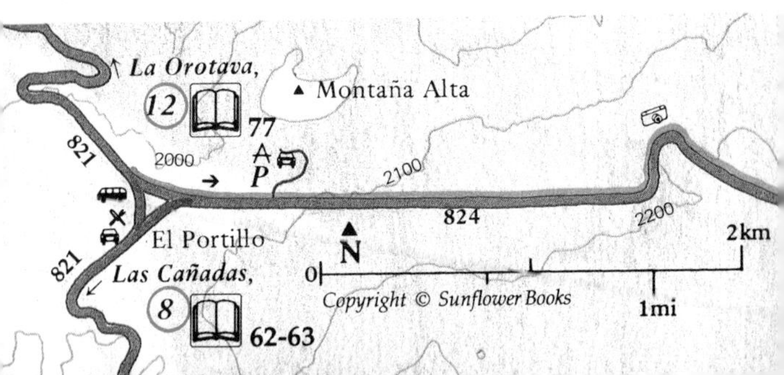

Continue down to La Caldera by taking the track that forks left and swings behind the shelter, dipping into a small flat area. A cairn stands at the turn-off. This is a very picturesque spot for a picnic. At about **5h35min** the track passes Galería Chimoche. Some five minutes later come to a T-junction: keep left downhill. Pass a water tank on the left (**6h**) and ignore the faint fork off to the right here. You pass another water tank on the left a few minutes later. La Caldera is now just minutes away.

On reaching the tarred road which circles La Caldera turn left: about 20m/yds downhill, on the right, take the small path down through tall heather (it's just opposite a wide track). It leads you to the car park and bus stop within a minute (**6h 20min**). Head for the bar/restaurant, if you have time to spare before your bus leaves.

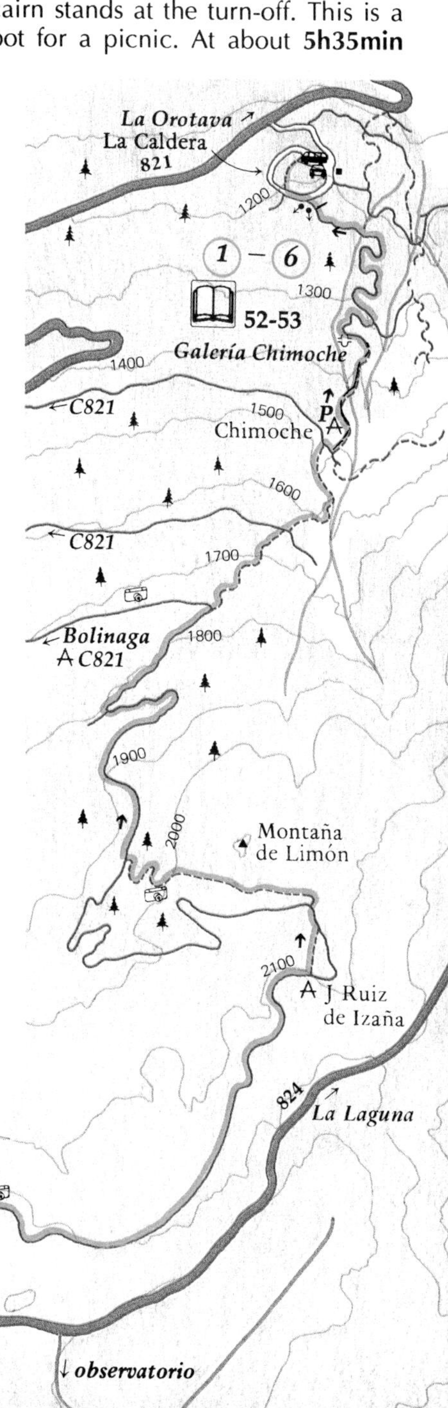

8 LAS CAÑADAS

See also photographs pages 17, 66-67

Distance: 18km/11.2mi; 4h45min

Grade: easy; hardly-perceptible climb of 200m/650ft; short descent

Equipment: stout shoes, long trousers *and* shorts, gloves, warm cardigans, anorak, raingear, sunhat, picnic, water

How to get there: 🚌 348 from Puerto to El Portillo (Timetable 5); journey time 1h20min

To return: 🚌 348 from the Parador de las Cañadas to Puerto (Timetable 5); journey time 2h15min

Alternative walk: Parador — Cañada de la Grieta — Parador: 11km/6.8mi; 4h; easy climb/descent of 100m/330ft; stout shoes, sunhat, picnic, water. To get there, and to begin this Alternative walk, use the notes for Walk 11, page 72. Follow Walk 11 as far as the turn-off for Guajara (1h), then continue along the track for another hour.

Few people will ever walk on the moon, but this ramble inside Tenerife's great volcanic crater, Las Cañadas*, must be a close approximation of the weird and awesome lunar landscape.

Tenerife has been a bed of volcanic activity for millennia. In fact, this activity is responsible for far more change on the island than are the elements. Controversy still exists about how the great crater of Las Cañadas was formed. One opinion claims that it is an enormous depression: Las Cañadas was originally covered by an dome. The collapse of the dome created the double crater which makes up this gigantic cauldron — the western side below the Roques de García and the eastern one stretching back to El Portillo. The other theory claims that erosion and the elements cut a large valley, opening to the north, and that this valley was later filled in by the surging up of El Teide and its off-sider, Chahorra. In either case, the crater was created some 300,000 years ago. The most recent activity here was a mere 200 years ago, when Chahorra (Pico Viejo) blew its top.

The following figures will give you some idea of the immensity of Las Cañadas: its diameter is almost 16km/10mi and its perimeter an astounding 45km/28mi. Much of it is surrounded by craggy, inconsistently-peaked walls, the highest point being Montaña de Guajara (Walk 11), 500m/1650ft above the floor of the

*The *cañadas* are plains of sedimentary rock or gravel (see photograph page 64), but the name 'Las Cañadas' is commonly applied to the crater in which these plains lie (see overview photograph pages 66-67).

crater but all of 2717m/ 8905ft above sea level. El Teide is the majestic centrepiece.

The trek begins at El Portillo's bar/restaurant. Walk up the road to the excellent Cañadas Visitors' Centre. Then follow the gravel track across the road from the Centre's car park. The track quickly disappears into arrogant, sharp terrain and spilled masses of rock. In **10min**, past a sharp curve to the left, keep right at a fork. A barrier will allow you into the protected zone. At this point the walls on your left are rather insignificant, and it's not obvious that you're inside a crater. The walls you follow form an arc. Smooth and perfectly-shaped scoria cones are evidence of former volcanic activity. The subtly-coloured *cañadas* give a touch of the desert. In winter these shallow gravelly plains often fill with water from melting snow.

At **45min**, the track begins to approach the escarpment

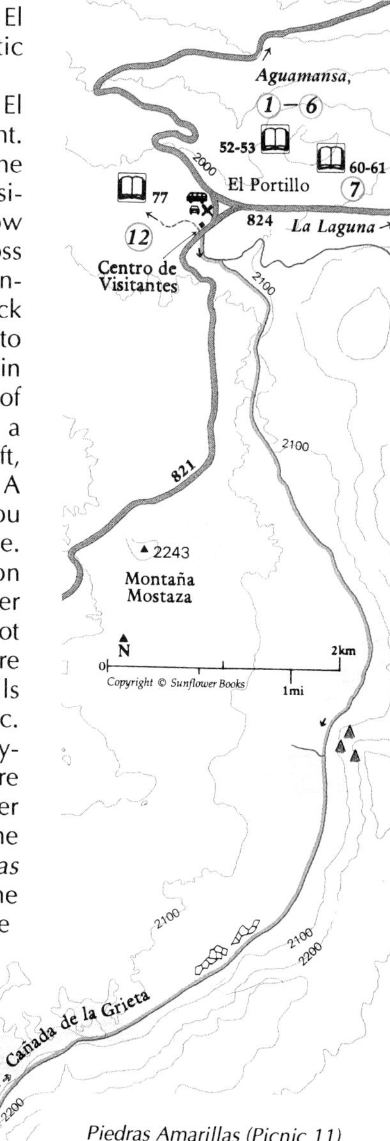

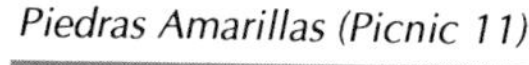

Piedras Amarillas (Picnic 11)

Retama and flaxweed brighten the way between the Visitors' Centre and Cañada de la Grieta. 'Rivers' of gravel flow around mounds of scoria below Montaña Blanca and El Teide (Walks 8, 9; Car tour 1).

walls. A perfectly-formed volcanic cone is seen ahead to the right; it's Montaña Mostaza. A beautiful tall wine-coloured rock formation on your left is passed at about **1h30min**. (Ignore a track to the right a few minutes later.) Later, after **2h**, an interesting rock formation of a different nature appears. Each rock has its own personality and seems to have been cut and shaped for its own particular niche in the jigsaw-like mounds. With the loose gravel beds forming inlets among them, Japanese rock gardens come to mind.

At **2h30min,** having crossed a small crest, an unexpected view awaits you: a large expanse of naked flat sediment — Cañada de la Grieta *(visited in the Alternative walk)*. Small crumbling animal pens sit in sheltered corners, a reminder of the days when the *cañadas* were grazed. A feeling of desolation hangs over the place, but in spring the *taginaste rojo,* the 'Pride of Tenerife', cheers the slopes on the left with its conical tower of close-knit, dashing red blooms.

The large flat-topped peak that has been shadowing you around the last few bends is Pico de Guajara (photograph page 72), and you pass the turn-off for the ascent at **3h45min**. Soon the bizarrely-sculpted Piedras Amarillas (Yellow Stones; photograph page 17) catch your eye, and you are at an unsurpassed viewing point for the western side of the crater. Beyond these rocks you join a tarred road. In half a minute, just past a pile of boulders, there is a short-cut on your right. Plunge in and find your way. Meet a track in five minutes; it takes you to the welcoming *parador* (**4h45min**).

9 EL TEIDE

NB: The summit of El Teide is not always accessible. It is open and closed at random. Enquire beforehand at the funicular station.

Distance: 8km/5mi; 6h *for the ascent;* 17km/10.5mi; 10h *return.*

Grade: ***very strenuous*** ascent and descent of 1367m/4485ft; however, the path is good. ***Take this walk very seriously:*** *Problems can include altitude sickness, no drinking water en route, and finding both the Refugio de Altavista and the funicular station at the summit closed.* Even if the funicular is operating at the start of the day, if a wind comes up it may be closed down, and you will have to descend on foot. Pay particular attention to the weather. Summer is obviously the best time for this hike. In winter don't attempt it if there is *even the most remote chance of bad weather.* I describe the walk as a one-way ascent to the summit and return by funicular — harder on the lungs, but easier on the legs than ascending by funicular and returning on foot. The best way to tackle this hike, however, is to climb to the Refugio de Altavista and spend the night there (details in advance from your local tourist information office). Early in the morning, make the final ascent (2h40min) to catch the sunrise, and descend by funicular or, preferably, on foot.

Equipment: walking boots, warm cardigans, anorak, sunhat, gloves, long trousers, thick socks, picnic, *plenty of water*

How to get there and return: 🚌 348 from Puerto to the Montaña Blanca turn-off and back (Timetable 5); journey time 1h35min. ***The average walker will not complete the walk in time to travel both ways by bus. You will have to arrange for friends or a taxi to take you to the start of the walk or collect you at the end.***

Short walk: C821 — Montaña Blanca — C821: 7km/4.3mi; 2h40min; moderate-strenuous ascent and descent of 400m/1300ft; equipment and access as above. Follow the main walk for 1h20min, then climb to the summit of Montaña Blanca. Return the same way.

There are not many high volcanic mountains where one can begin the assault at well over halfway up. In fact, a bus will drop you at the 2350 metre-mark. Another plus is that you needn't be a mountaineer to tackle this climb: from bottom to top, there's an easy-to-follow path. *But you must be **very fit.*** Among the problems you may encounter is altitude sickness — the signs usually being nausea and a headache. This often results when ascending too quickly. A slower ascent, with frequent rests, may relieve your sickness but, if it persists, it's best to turn back. *Take heed, too, of the warnings under 'Grade' above.*

El Teide is the result of numerous volcanic eruptions.

Below the summit of El Teide, at the edge of a small crater

Chahorra, to the west of El Teide, was probably the most significant, and El Pilón (the peak itself) is still active. El Pilón rose over an older and much larger crater called La Rambleta, which lies just to the left of the funicular station near the summit.

We start out at the Montaña Blanca turn-off, where the bus stops. Follow the track towards Montaña Blanca. The landscape here — blanketed in pumice and scoria, interrupted by the occasional patch of jagged rock, wallows in desolation (see photograph page 64). Some **20min** from the bus stop, you have a choice: you can take a short cut by following the second small path on the left (the beginning involves scrambling over loose, sharp scoria). You will meet the track again in about 25 minutes; follow it uphill to the left. Or, if you want to save your breath for the major part of the climb, just keep to the track. In either case, don't forget to look behind you at the unique view. In the Cañadas lie what look like rough mounds of chocolate. The walls clearly delineate the limits of the crater. The Las Cañadas Visitors' Centre is but a few daubs of white.

At **1h** (**1h20min**, if you followed the track) come to an old car park (2750m/9000ft). It's just a short walk from here to Montaña Blanca's summit. But for those of you ascending El Teide, this is where the real climbing begins. A large sign for the Refugio de Altavista points you towards a partially-collapsed, pen-like construction, at the right of which the ascent begins. The sandy

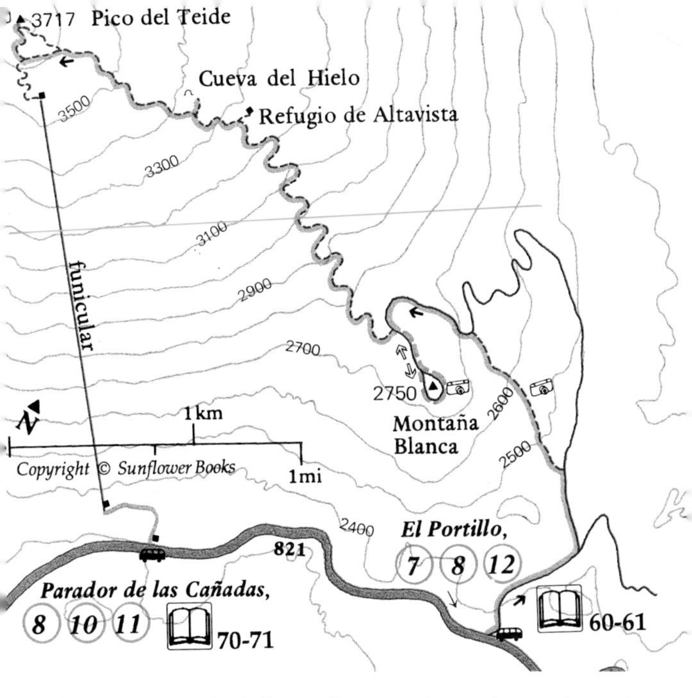

path is very easily followed. From down here, the side of El Teide seems to be split vertically: the left is clothed in dark lava flow and the right in light crusty pumice.

At **3h20min** the *refugio* is no longer a dot on the mountainside. You're there, 3270m/10,725ft up. The refuge is *usually* open from 17.00 to 10.00. Your path continues up behind the shelter, to the left, through a landscape covered in stones and chunks of rock. Half an hour up from the *refugio*, turn off right at a signpost for 'Cueva del Hielo'. This 15-minute detour takes you over and into a large, sunken cave. A springy metal ladder allows you to enter this den. *Do so with care.* Inside the cave are many stalactites of hanging ice.

Returning to the main path (**4h20min**), the smooth volcanic cone of Montaña Mostaza (Walk 8) stands out below. Steel poles along the route indicate the way to the summit. Soon the walk levels out a bit. If a wind is blowing, as it often is, this is where it will be in full force. It can easily knock you off balance. Quickly come to a T-junction,

Las Cañadas from the summit of El Teide. Gran Canaria rises in the distance above a sea of clouds.

where a right turn leads to a viewpoint half a minute along. The main walk bears left here (**5h**) and the way becomes a rock-paved path twisting through a wild sea of rock. Not far up, the funicular station comes into view. You join the path that leads from the funicular to the vertex, by a sign 'Keep this way please'. Rising puffs of steam betray concealed holes in the ground. Whiffs of sulphur waft by. If your hands need warming, hold them over these steaming holes. The drop in temperature causes small droplets of condensation, and strings of frozen water crystallise on the rocks; when the sun's rays catch these droplets, the slope appears diamond-studded.

At **5h30min** you'll come to the setting shown on page 65: a small crater (80m/yds diameter) just below the peak. Here the soft colours of an ice cream parlour surround you: peach melba, banana, strawberry, mocha, pistachio. On a clear day, your view will encompass four islands — La Gomera, Gran Canaria, El Hierro and La Palma.

A 20-minute descent on the same path takes you to the funicular station and a warm bar (**6h**). To return to Montaña Blanca on foot, go back to the joining of the *refugio* path and the final descent path. Five minutes past the old car park, on a sharp U-bend, you can pick up the short-cut path you may have taken earlier (**10h**).

10 ROQUES DE GARCIA • CUEVAS DE LOS ROQUES • ROQUES DE GARCIA

Distance: 4.5km/2.8mi; 2h **See also photograph page 72**

Grade: gentle climb and descent of 200m/650ft

Equipment: stout shoes (boots preferable), sunhat, cardigans, anorak, raingear, gloves, picnic, water

How to get there: 🚌 348 from Puerto to the Parador de Las Cañadas (Timetable 5); journey time 2h15min

To return: 🚌 348 from the *parador* to Puerto (as above)

Getting to know the Cañadas takes time. There's so much to see. Here's a suggestion for a short hike into the quieter, less-visited realms of this great cauldron. It focuses on caves formed millennia ago by the lava streams of various volcanic eruptions. These caves, sixteen in all, are housed in an area of *pahoehoe* (ropey lava; see photograph page 70). The lava flow is usually a smooth stream of distorted, rolling hillocks and hollows; parts of it resemble cord, or coils of rope — hence the name. The ropey lava flow is formed on the thin crust of the stream, either by the movement of liquified lava underneath, or by the sliding of the crust where it has thrust up into a hillock. The more common lava up here is the 'A-A' (block lava) — large scoriaceous masses of jagged, fragmented rock.

Start out at the *parador* and make your way over to the Roques de García (Picnic 10) which lie across the main road, a five-minute walk away. Before starting up towards the caves, be sure to visit the *mirador* looking over into Cañada Llano de Ucanca. The gigantic fractured rock rising up in front of you, out of this *cañada,* is called La Catedral. Steps on your right take you within five minutes to a good view into this row of eroded beauties.

To continue the walk, all you have to do is keep this line of eroded rocks on your left. Five minutes uphill your wide path heads off through *retama* (it's just to the left of the path to the old WCs, which are now closed).

The weirdly-formed Roques de García, with El Teide in the background (Walk 10, Picnic 10, Car tour 1)

Pahoehoe lava (the name is Hawaiian) comes underfoot as you approach the Roques Blancos. The mass, which resembles freshly-poured batter, is your ongoing path to the Cuevas de los Roques.

Within **30min** the way narrows, as it passes between a ridge of rough, jagged rock on your right and the Roques on your left. You will notice two jagged rocky upthrusts on your right on the way up, close on **35min**. *Keep these in mind as a reference point for later in the walk.*

Lumps of *pahoehoe* lava begin coming underfoot as you approach the Roques Blancos, the last of the Roques de García. La Torre Blanca (the White Tower) is a solitary rock upthrust met at the **45min**-mark. Here is where you mount this mass of easily-recognised ropey lava. At the far end of La Torre Blanca, head straight up the middle of the lava run. White paint markers are visible on the left-hand side of the lava flow; the flow itself is your path. All the caves open out of it. They were formed when the surface crust thickened but the lava underneath continued to run, spreading its tentacles. When these streams subsided, they left an extensive network of tunnels and caves.

After about 10 minutes up the flow, start to look out for a small cairn on a hillock of lava. The first cave is just to the left of it — downhill a bit and marked with the number 5. It is in line with Torre Blanca. You're now about **1h05min** into the walk. This is a small cave, and the mouth of it only allows you to squeeze in. A passage disappears down into the dark. Rough small pinnacles hang from the ceiling like stalactites. About five minutes up you find the next cave; it's slightly to the right of the first one. As before, a cairn marks it. This is one of the larger caves, extending some 1000m/3300ft back into the slope. The caves are actually quite hard to find, as they are not signposted, and there are no convenient landmarks. If you have trouble finding them, here's a tip: looking back down the course of the walk from here, you will see two small rocks (the ones mentioned earlier). Now find the chapel beside the *parador.* To locate the exact spot of this second cave, the chapel must appear dead centre between those two rocks. Another cave lies behind this second one, and straight up from these two, just three minutes away, hides another.

At this point, you are approaching the top of the lava flow. The last cave, another large one, is nearby — uphill to your left (**1h15min**). A hole in the ground leads you down into the entrance. If it's windy, the open back section of the cave is a good picnic spot/solarium. El Teide is just beside you now, and Guajara stands out quite grandly in the crater wall.

Heading back downhill, the route is very straightforward, unless you're enveloped by mist. If this should happen, just keep to the left-hand side (facing downhill) of the lava stream and, at the bottom, the rocks will guide you back to the main road and bus stop (**2h**).

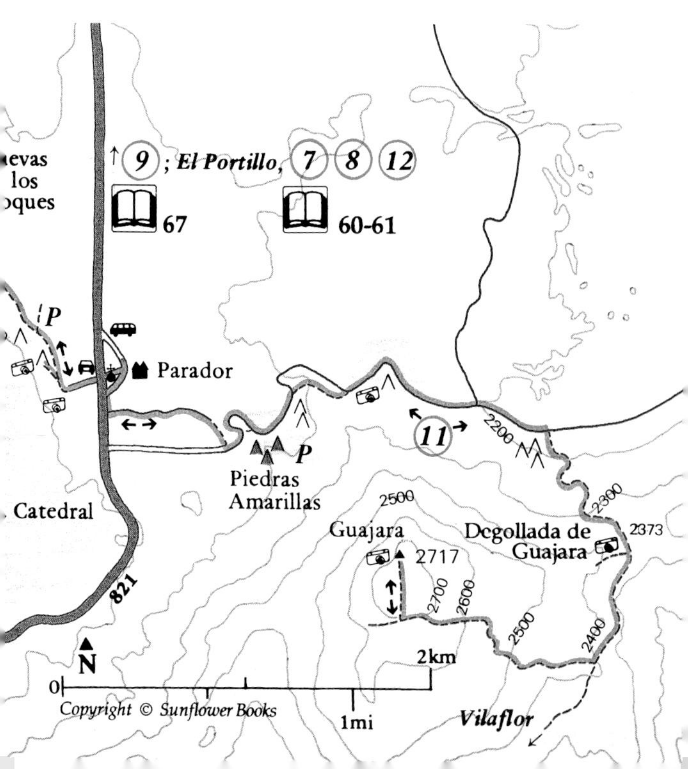

11 MONTAÑA DE GUAJARA

Map page 71; see also photographs pages 17 and 63

Distance: 13km/8mi; 5h

Grade: moderate climb and *somewhat slippery* descent of 600m/1950ft; *do not attempt in uncertain weather.*

Equipment: stout shoes (boots preferable), sunhat, cardigans, anorak, long trousers, gloves, thick socks, picnic, water

How to get there: 🚌 348 from Puerto to the Parador de las Cañadas (Timetable 5); journey time 2h15min
To return: 🚌 348 from the *parador* to Puerto (as above)

Shorter walk: Parador — Degollada de Guajara — Parador: 8.5km/5.3mi; 3h10min; easy-moderate climb and descent of under 250m/820ft; access/equipment as above. Follow the main walk for 1h40min; return the same way. Map page 71.

Guajara is Tenerife's third highest mountain, standing at 2717m/8910ft. This is an easy, straightforward climb, offering superb views down into the crater of Las Cañadas. As you ascend Guajara's back, the southern coastal plain unravels in a haze below.

Start out at the *parador.* Head for the main road, past the chapel, and turn left (south). After 50m/yds along the main road, meet a gravel track on your left. Follow it until it fades (**10min**). Veer right alongside the rocky ridge and look for a line of loosely-spaced rocks. This will guide you to a tarred road in a few minutes. Turn left and, within a minute, you pass through the control barrier into the Las Cañadas track. A fascinating formation of pink and yellow rocks rises just in front of you. The mellow colours give this fine natural sculpture its name — Piedras Amarillas ('Yellow Stones'; Picnic 11; photograph page 17). Behind them, a small *cañada* (gravel plain; see photograph page 64) will be your first introduction to many more along the way. At the **35min**-mark you pass through another *cañada* with cone-shaped rocks on the right. Here Guajara — the bastion of the encircling walls — is seen at its best, rising 500m/1650ft from the crater floor. Splashes of

Guajara from the Roques de García. The Piedras Amarillas and the 'Chapel of the Snows' are dwarfed beneath the peak (Picnic 10, Walk 11, Car tour 1).

yellow lichen, like paint daubs, decorate the higher rock faces. In spring, *taginaste rojo* — some as tall as 3m/10ft — adds bold strokes of red to this canvas.

Your ascent begins at the **1h**-mark. *Attention:* it's not very obvious. It lies not far beyond a turn-off to the left, and about 70m/yds past a bend in the track dominated by a towering wall of rock. Your only landmark is a small cairn on the right-hand side of the track. Turn up right. The path is clear and easy to follow, waymarked with white arrows, dots and, nearer the summit, numbers — a 'countdown' starting at 22.

At **1h40min**, you reach the edge of the crater at the Degollada (Pass) de Guajara (2373m/7785ft). The views are magnificent. The tones are the most dramatic aspect of this landscape, as they flow into and across each other. A metal pole and various signs on rocks mark this pass, *from where the Shorter walk turns back.*

Ignore the small path branching off right at the pass: a red arrow shows your way, beneath bleached pumice cliffs on your right. Gran Canaria seems surprisingly close from this vantage point. At **1h55min**, after a brief ascent, the path forks: a red arrow points right (to Guajara) and a white one left to Vilaflor.* There may also be a metal pole here. Keep right uphill. An eroded watercourse becomes your path. In places, you'll have to rely on waymarking dots to show the way. A few minutes up, a large rock on the right with two dots should confirm it. Number 8 in the countdown comes up at about **2h30min.** The way eases out as it swings across the *retama*- and *codéso*-patched slope. Around here the path fades from time to time, so be prepared to search out the waymarking dots (usually white) .

El Teide slowly reappears until it is seen in its full magnificence when you reach the Guajara summit (**3h**), marked by a concrete pole. There's also a rock enclosure here — a good picnic shelter on a windy winter's day. The panorama from Guajara's summit can only be matched by that from El Teide; in fact, from here, there's an even better perspective over the Cañadas.

The return path begins a little to the left of the rock-pen. While your descent is much easier, take it very slowly down the slippery stretch of pumice (**5h**).

*The Vilaflor path passes by the famous 'moon landscape'. This hike is described in a companion volume, *Landscapes of Southern Tenerife and La Gomera.*

12 EL PORTILLO • PIEDRA DE LOS PASTORES • GALERIA ALMAGRE Y CABEZON • CHANAJIGA • PALO BLANCO

Distance: 14.5km/9mi; 4h30min **See also photograph page 59**

Grade: moderate-strenuous descent of 1450m/4750ft; some sections are very steep and *hazardous if wet.*

Equipment: stout shoes (boots preferable), cardigans, anorak, sunhat, raingear, picnic, water

How to get there: 🚌 348 from Puerto to El Portillo (Timetable 5); journey time 1h20min
To return: 🚌 347 from Palo Blanco to La Orotava (Timetable 10); journey time 30min; *change to* 🚌 350 to Puerto (Timetable 3); journey time 30min

Short walk: El Portillo — Choza Cruz de Fregel — El Portillo: 7km/4.3mi; 2h15min; easy descent and ascents totalling under 200m/650ft; equipment as above, but stout shoes will suffice. Return from El Portillo on 🚌 348 (as above). Follow the main walk for 1h05min and return the same way.

Three stretches of beauty make this walk: the volcanic world that lies at the foot of El Teide, the sea of fine gravel just before you leave it, and the lush trails that descend the slopes to Chanajiga.

On your bus journey up to El Portillo, you'll pass the famous Margarita de Piedra — a basaltic rock formation in the shape of a daisy (drawing page 12). You are also likely to see enormous piles of pine needles alongside the road, awaiting collection. They're laid in animal pens or used as packing material for the easily-bruised fruit.

Leave the bus at El Portillo and walk along the road to the Las Cañadas Visitors' Centre (open 09.00-16.00). This is where **your trail begins**. Set off on the neatly-landscaped path shown opposite; it goes round the left-hand side of the building (as you face it). In two minutes meet a path and turn left, heading towards El Teide. Keep right at a fork met in about five minutes and pass a turn-off right 10 minutes later. This park-like walk (Picnic 12b) ends in **25min**: on joining a rough narrow track, bear right. From here you get a good view of the Roque del Peral on your left. Ignore all turn-offs along this track.

An exciting change takes place as you descend to an unexpected, sunken 'lake' of fine-gravelled pumice and sand. At **55min**, your feet will assure you it's not solely sand — as it at first appears. This is Cañada de los Guancheros, and you almost feel as though you have made a discovery — until footprints and, later on, a two-wheeled track makes themselves obvious. Cross the *cañada* keeping near the right-hand wall. Five minutes across, beyond a blade of rock jutting out of the wall, climb a hillside path to a small cluster of pines that huddle in a pass to the right of La Fortaleza. Here you come upon Choza Cruz de Fregel (**1h05min**; photograph page 59). Three wooden crosses sit in a small shrine at this picnic spot, where tables, benches and barbecues are laid out under the pines.

From here follow the forestry track to the right. Pass a turn-off climbing to the left but take the *next* forestry track branching off left; *sendero turístico* signs confirm the way. For much of its course, this forestry track is too rough to be motorable. Ten minutes further down, you cross a U-bend in the track you were originally following, and ten minutes later this track is crossed again. Continue straight downhill. Ignore the forestry track alongside you.

A wide fire-break on the western side of this ridge is met at **1h50min**. It leads to La Corona, above Icod el

The park-like path leading to the Cañada de los Guancheros (Picnic 12b, Car tours 1 and 5)

Alto (Walk 13). At this point you join a track coming from the right and continue downhill through the frayed clearing, with some striking views over the whole Orotava Valley.

A small, pretty shrine marks **2h10min**. Ten minutes later come to Choza Piedra de los Pastores (the Shepherds' Rock Shelter, but there is no longer any shelter, only a table and a bench). Here signs point in all directions. Bear right on a track for 'Fuente de Mesa/Portillo'. This track is in very good condition — definitely motorable. This is another good viewing point overlooking the carpet of inconsistent green forest stretching to the right and the arable squares of farmlands stepped to the coast. Some 15 minutes along the track, watch for a narrow path cutting off to your left: there are *no signs* marking it, but it's about 50m/yds past wide parking bays on either side of the track. Descend this path. Heather, a few pines, and moss-covered rocks keep the route fresh in greens. The descent is steep and slippery; watch your footing!

At **2h50min** a pleasant *galería* (see page 40) greets you as you come out onto a forestry track — Galería Almagre y Cabezón. Flowering bushes and flower-beds make this a good picnic spot — when the motor isn't running! There's even a table with benches. This water gallery sits in front of a rocky embankment.

From here take the forestry track to the left (at the bottom of the path you've just descended). Pass a turn-off to the right, signposted 'Zona Recreativa Chanajiga/ Cruz de Luís/Aguamansa'. Beyond here, *take care* not to miss your turn-off to the right, about 20 minutes down the track from the *galería.* A beehive of rocks, with a yellow *sendero turístico* sign on it, alerts you to to this path to Chanajiga. With the aroma of pines following you and the forsaken old buildings along the way, this path comes as quite a change. At about **3h20min**, you'll come upon an old watercourse, chuckling away to itself. It leads you round a verdant bend in the path and straight to an abandoned old water gallery — Galería La Zarza.

At about **3h30min** branch left down to the Chanajiga picnic area (the first left turn you encounter). Have a picnic, perhaps, in the story-book setting of wooden bridges, rustic tables and benches (Picnic 12a). It's about an hour from here to Palo Blanco (**4h30min**): use the notes for Walk 13 from the 4h-point, on page 79.

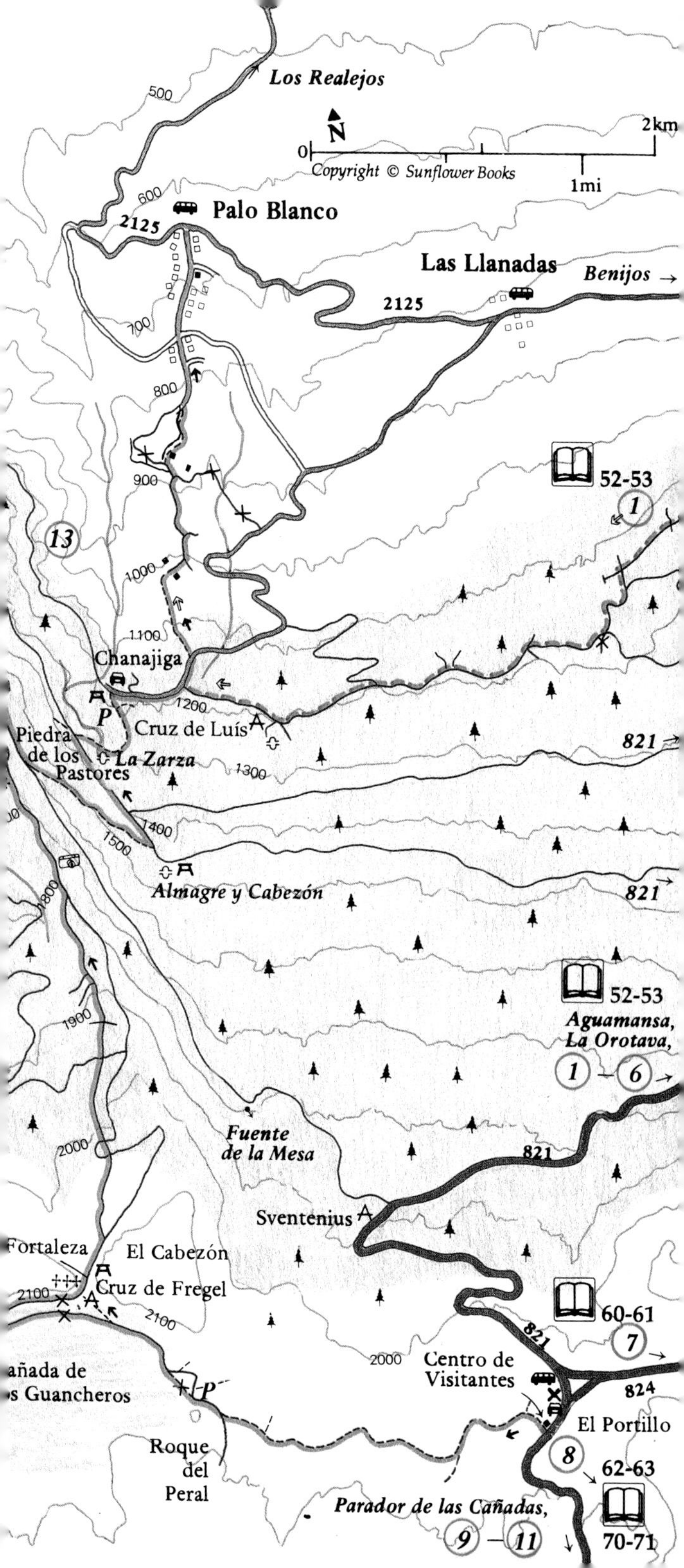
Los Realejos
N
0
2km
1mi
Copyright © Sunflower Books
Palo Blanco
2125
Las Llanadas
Benijos →
500
600
700
800
900
1000
1100
1200
1300
1400
1500
1800
1900
2000
2100
52-53
1
13
Chanajiga
P
Cruz de Luís
Piedra de los Pastores
La Zarza
821
Almagre y Cabezón
52-53
Aguamansa, La Orotava,
1 – 6
Fuente de la Mesa
Sventenius
Fortaleza
El Cabezón
Cruz de Fregel
Cañada de los Guancheros
Roque del Peral
60-61
7
Centro de Visitantes
824
El Portillo
8
62-63
Parador de las Cañadas,
9 – 11
70-71

13 ICOD EL ALTO • LA CORONA • CHANAJIGA • PALO BLANCO

Distance: 10.5km/6.5mi; 5h (or 5h30min to Los Realejos)

Grade: strenuous, with an initial climb of 700m/2300ft and a steep descent of 600m/2000ft

Equipment: stout shoes (walking boots preferable), cardigan, anorak, sunhat, raingear, picnic, water

How to get there: 🚌 354 from Puerto to Icod el Alto (Timetable 4); journey time 35min
To return: 🚌 347 from Palo Blanco to La Orotava (Timetable 10); journey time 30min; *change to* 🚌 350 to Puerto (Timetable 3); journey time 30min

Shorter walk: Icod — Mirador El Asomadero — Icod: 6km/3.8mi; 4h; moderate-strenuous ascent/descent of 500m/1650ft. Follow the main walk for 2h10min; return the same way for 🚌 354 to Puerto.

If you've done Walk 4, you've explored the Orotava Valley from the east. On this walk, you'll get to know the west. This trek is one continuous panorama, where your views stretch far beyond the eastern escarpment. The hike ascends a ridge. A lovely picnic spot, Chanajiga, awaits you near the end. And then the rural descent lets you absorb the country atmosphere and appreciate the farmers' handiwork.

On the bus journey to Icod, you have an opportunity to see one of the big dragon trees. This one stands on the opposite side of the ravine, just out of Los Realejos.

Press the button after the first bus stop in Icod el Alto, which is just beyond the Mirador de El Lance. Your stop is the *next* one. Off the bus, cross the road. Walk downhill (right) to a bus shelter: 15m/yds beyond it, climb the wide lane (for pedestrians only) between the houses. It brings you onto a road rising steeply off the TF221.

Start the walk by huffing and puffing your way uphill on this road. You leave Icod quickly. On joining the tarred La Corona road, turn left. In under 10 minutes you reach a turn-off left to the Mirador de La Corona (**1h**; Picnic 13), where there is a shrine and a restaurant. The view from here is a sample of what lies further up. Once you've absorbed it all, and worked out where each village lies, head up the ridge. From here, a wide, dusty farm and forestry track leads you straight up. Don't take any of the tracks that turn off across the hillside, over to your right. (If you are ever in doubt, always follow the *edge* of the ridge.)

At **1h20min**, at an intersection, continue straight uphill. You head up an overgrown fire-break. From here on, this fire-break is your guide. All along the rim of this escarpment, you'll have great picture-postcard views of the Orotava Valley. At **1h40min** (at the 900m contour on the map) meet a forestry track which completes its curve and veers off to the right. Another, smaller track heads off left round the eastern face of the ridge. Keep between these two tracks and take the next track off to the left (the remains of the fire-break). There's a water tank not far up on your left. A little further on, a solitary forestry house comes into view on the right. At about **2h** you join the main forestry track on a bend, then immediately leave it by forking left on another track that cuts up the edge of the escarpment. (The main track now winds up through scrub, over on your right.)

Another magnificent viewpoint, the Mirador El Asomadero, will draw you to a halt at **2h10min**. You're overlooking farmland, a quilted patchwork of fields in the upper valley. Straight in front of you is Palo Blanco, an elongated rural settlement, clearly identified by the school. *The Shorter walk turns back here.* Five minutes later, reach an intersection, some 20m/yds beyond a trail on the left. (This trail is shown in green on the map, but is now overgrown: an X on the map indicates 'wrong way'.) Keep left uphill. Three minutes later meet another intersection and again keep left. When you next meet the main track, follow it uphill to the right. A couple of minutes later, leave the main track again: head left uphill. This brings you to an important junction, where you again bear left. From here on, clear views accompany you all the way to Chanajiga (**4h**), where Walk 12 comes in (from Piedra de los Pastores).

To make for Palo Blanco, follow the gravel road downhill for 300m/yds, to a signposted junction. Turn left here on a tarred road. About 100m/yds downhill, on a curve, you'll come to a cairn on your left. Turn left off the road and follow this wide, stony path. As you're walking down, look up to your left and see the track that brought you down the mountainside (it's the lower one). A minute past two concrete farm sheds you join a gravel farm track. Bear left and continue downhill. At

From the Corona Mirador your view stretches across the Orotava Valley (Picnic 13; detour on Car tour 3)

4h25min pass straight through a junction of tracks. Always keep straight downhill. At **4h40min** turn right on a concrete drive. The way soon becomes tarred. This very steep descent takes you through authentic rural landscape, with hidden courtyards, flower-beds, children and dogs galore. Pass the school on the right and continue down to the main road, which cuts in front of you (**5h**). Just uphill on the left is a shop, and the bus stop is in front of it. Buses here in Palo Blanco are infrequent. But if you continue straight over the road, half an hour downhill, in Los Realejos, you can pick up a bus to Puerto. (When you come to a street with shops, veer right, then take the first left: the bus stop is just past the police station.)

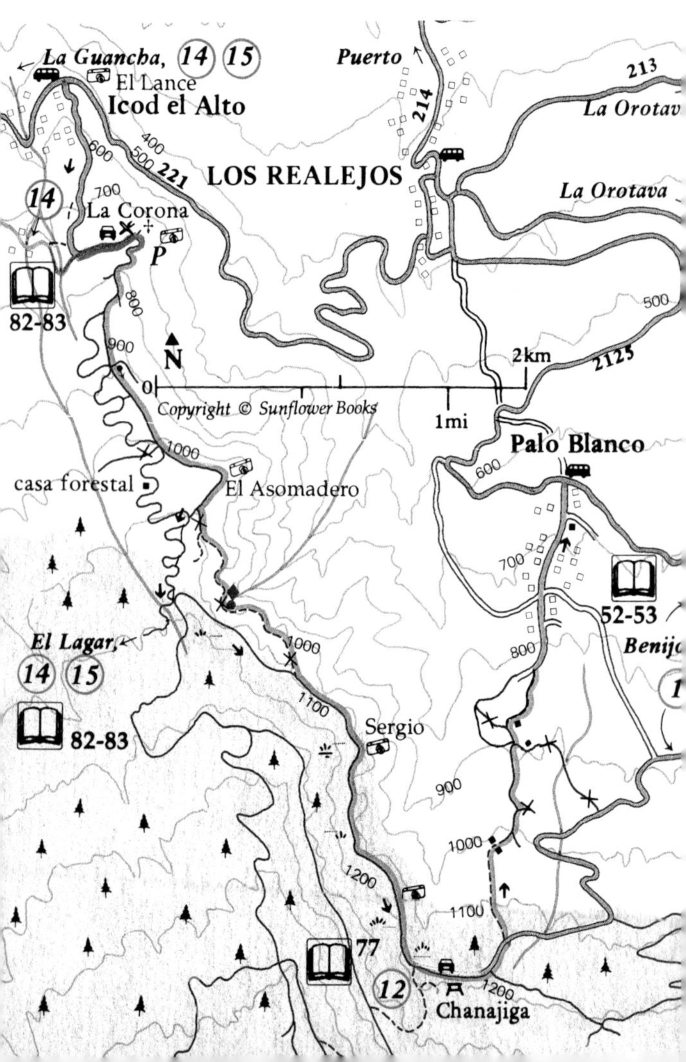

14 ICOD EL ALTO • EL LAGAR • LA GUANCHA

Distance: 18km/11.2mi; 9h05min **See also photograph page 89**

Grade: very strenuous and long, with a steep ascent of 1000m/3300ft at the start and a descent of 1000m/3300ft at the end. To avoid the initial climb, take a taxi to El Lagar and use the map to walk from there to Icod (ie, do the walk in reverse).

Equipment: stout shoes (walking boots preferable in wet weather), sunhat, cardigans, anorak, long trousers, raingear, picnic, water

How to get there: 🚌 354 from Puerto to Icod el Alto (Timetable 4); journey time 35min

To return: 🚌 354 from La Guancha to Puerto (as above)

Shorter walk: Icod el Alto — bridge — Icod el Alto: 8km/5mi; 6h30min; strenuous climb/descent of 800m/2600ft; equipment and access as above; return on the same bus. Follow the main walk to the 4h-point and return the same way.

High terraced slopes, rich in cultivation, lead you higher still, into the confines of the forest. On this walk, contact with Canarians is a certainty. They will be only too happy to know where you're from and where you are going. If a laden apple tree is nearby, your pockets will surely be filled.

Press the button after the first bus stop in Icod el Alto, which is just beyond the Mirador de El Lance. Your stop is the *next* one. Off the bus, cross the road. Walk downhill (right) to a bus shelter: 15m/yds beyond it, climb the wide lane (for pedestrians only) between the houses. It brings you onto a road rising steeply off the TF221.

Start the walk by huffing and puffing your way uphill on this road. You leave Icod quickly. In under **45min** a small hamlet sits on the nose of a ridge over to your right. At this point, take the narrow path on the right (about 20m/yds beyond the last house, on a bend in the road). In **55min** cross the tarred road leading to the Mirador La Corona and head up the steep road almost opposite. This road soon reverts to track and runs along a ridge of rich alluvial plots.

Forty minutes up this track, a confusion of tracks confronts you: take the track immediately to the right, heading for a lone farmhouse. Some minutes along, turn left up another track, going towards the house (a short cut). Then rejoin the main track, which heads almost straight uphill to the La Guancha forestry track. Montaña de Taco, a volcanic cone rising out of Buenavista's coastal plain, can be seen from here. On clear days La Palma is visible on the horizon.

As you climb, ignore a track branching off to the right. Ten minutes later, you come to a series of turn-offs. Take the third turn-off to the left and head straight uphill on a rough, disused track. During the next 20 minutes, ignore two more turn-offs. El Teide is before you, rising above the pines, and heather cloaks the immediate slopes.

Within **4h** reach the La Guancha forestry track and turn right into a particularly lovely corner of the forest, where there is a quaint high bridge. *(The Shorter walk turns back from this point.)* You will now follow this track, without turning off. Pass over an old watercourse and, from here on, you should be alongside a large water pipe which follows this main track. Pass a fork off to the right and then cross straight over an intersection (**4h 15min**). A small shrine, full of flowers, is

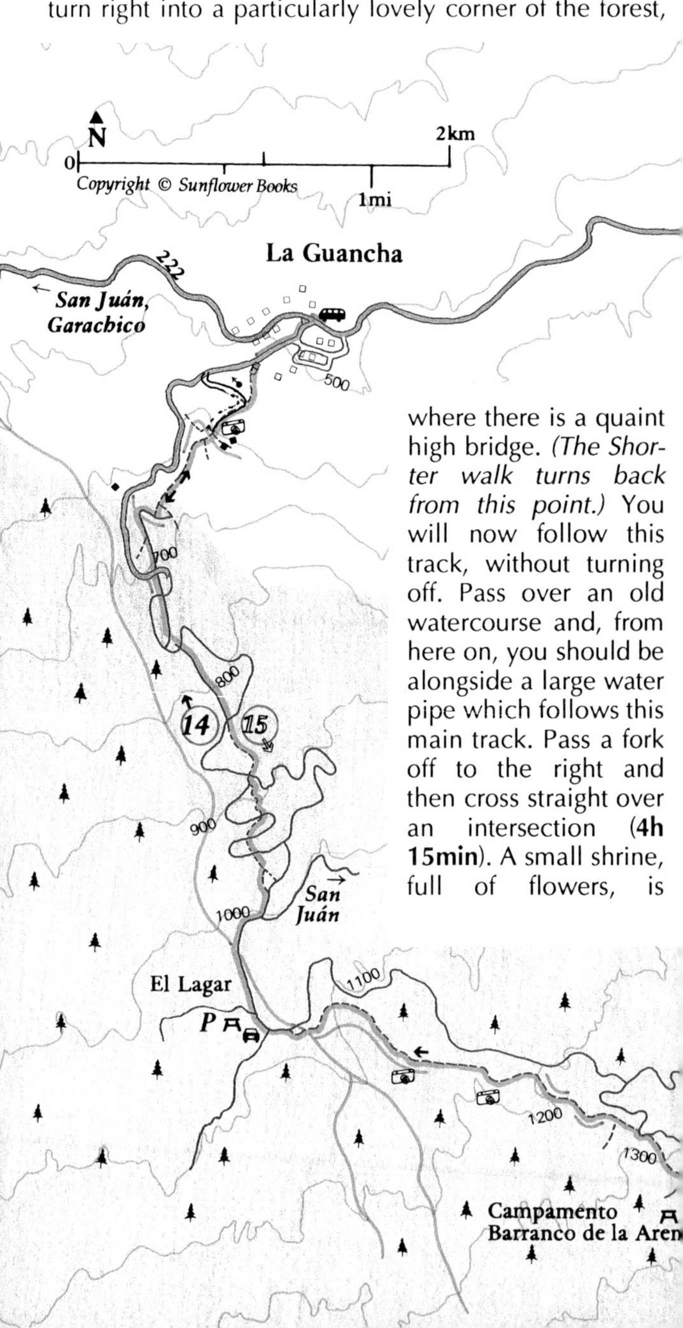

passed within **5h40min**. Over five minutes later, ignore the turn-off to the right.

Somewhat over two hours' walking along this forestry track (at about **6h10min**), you meet a track descending from Galería Vergara Baja (Walk 15). Keep right here. At about this point you part company with the water pipe, which now cuts across the hillside. A few minutes later a track joins from the right; keep left. Two minutes later pass through a major junction and keep straight on for El Lagar and La Guancha. You come to Campamento Barranco de la Arena, a campsite and picnic area (**6h 25min**).

Leaving the campsite, follow the track that cuts *through* the

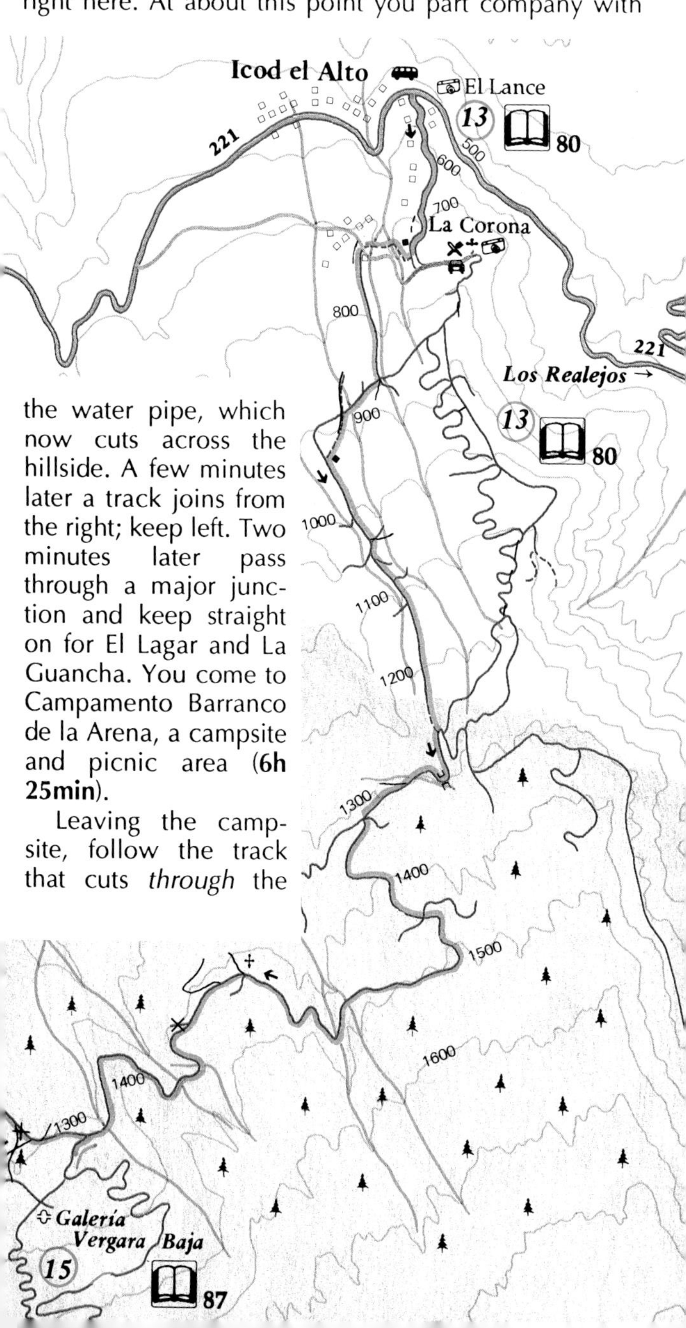

Between Campamento Barranco de la Arena and El Lagar (Picnic 14, Walks 14 and 15)

picnic grounds (*not* the track running to the right of the grounds). A few minutes along you leave through a barrier and meet a track coming from the left. Cross over the track and, some 20m/yds along, on your right, take the path forking down to the left, through rocks and into the pines. In ten minutes you rejoin the track. Descend it for a minute and then rejoin your path, heading left and back into the woods. Ignore all the faint turn-offs; keep straight downhill. The track and path run parallel with each other from time to time, and a small water pipe accompanies you. Then the somewhat-overgrown path rises, nestling into the slope of a ridge. Shortly you cross another low ridge: ahead of you is a superb panorama and, behind, you can see the forestry watchtower and the back of La Fortaleza (Walk 12). The path descends away from the pipe. Another superb view beckons ten minutes later, as you begin to descend the left-hand side of a steep ridge. El Teide dominates the waves of pines. When you eventually rejoin the track, follow it down to the left, then bear right.

The El Lagar *zona recreativa* (**7h40min**; Picnic 14) is 100m/yds below. From here you will follow the track for a few minutes, but then woodcutters' paths will take you to the beautifully-sited village of La Guancha, strung along a ridge. Start down the track from El Lagar. Eight minutes downhill, pass by the San Juán/Los Realejos turn-off (on the right). Five minutes later, rounding a sweeping bend, you'll see a ridge sloping down to the left. Take the path running along the top of it. (If you miss this turn-off, you'll have another opportunity to join the path some 50m/yds downhill.) On crossing the forestry track, find your path immediately opposite. Several minutes later, you cross the track again: the path continues slightly to your right. Cross the track again in two minutes and continue downhill through a particularly scenic part of the forest (the path is slightly overgrown here). You leave the woodland path again at a junction: almost exactly at the point where the two tracks meet, your path re-enters the wood (you have to clamber up a small embankment). Continue downhill into the bottom of a shallow gulley. Passing this way late in the afternoon, you'll appreciate the streams of light flickering through the dark shadows.

You leave the shady pine forest and cross the track into a nursery of pines. An obviously-disused track takes over from the path. Ten minutes downhill, another track is crossed. Here veer slightly left onto an old forestry track and, 10m/yds along it, you will find your path again, dipping off to the right. The path joins an old track, and the gurgle of fast-running water from a *canal* announces your next track crossing. Go down through trees and moss.

You meet a tarred road in under **8h30min**. Cross it and continue through pines and heather. A little way along this track, ignore the path branching off to the left. A *canal* passes below you, as the track bends to the right. A minute later, on your left, a small gap in the dense vegetation opens onto a rocky path. Follow it to another, wider path which takes you above cultivated plots. Thick, tightly-woven moss carpets the shady corners of this path. The forest continues down past you on the left. The road is below, and the town of La Guancha is at last near. The sea is glistening over the pines. Enjoy these final far-reaching coastal views.

You meet a junction about 15 minutes down the path (**8h45min**). This is a very picturesque spot. Two rustic dwellings sit on the crest of this ridge, guarding their plots below. Descend the concrete lane on your right, through wine country. Clusters of white dwellings come into sight as they extend across the face of the escarpment and dribble down the ridges. Five minutes down the concrete lane, on a sharp bend, fork right on a path (just when you are above a large circular water tank). Keep right and come to a basketball court. Turn left to the tarred road. The main road can be seen from here, passing through the town centre. To get there, turn right down the road, go left at the T-junction and, three minutes later, a flight of steps on your left will take you there. Turn right on the main road. The bus stop is some 200m/yds ahead, outside the Camara Agraria Local (**9h05min**).

15 CAMPAMENTO BARRANCO DE LA ARENA • CANAL VERGARA • EL LAGAR • LA VEGA

See map opposite to begin, map on pages 82-83 to continue, and sketch map on pages 88-89 to end the walk; see also photo page 84

Distance: 21.5km/13.4mi; 7h10min

Grade: moderate-strenuous. There is an initial climb and descent of 200m/650ft, another descent of 200m/650ft, and a final descent of 500m/1650ft; in between the route is level, but long.

Equipment: stout shoes or walking boots, sunhat, cardigans, anorak, raingear, picnic, water

How to get there: 354 from Puerto to La Guancha (Timetable 4); journey time 45min; taxi from La Guancha to Campamento Barranco de la Arena
To return: 360 from La Vega to Icod de los Vinos (Timetable 8); journey time 35min, or 359 from La Vega to Icod de los Vinos (not in the timetables): daily departures at 14.00, 16.05, 17.30, 19.20; *change to* 363 from Icod to Puerto (Timetable 6); journey time 45min

Alternative, shorter walks:

1 Campamento Barranco de la Arena — Icod el Alto: 11.5km/7.1mi; 4h10min; moderate ascent of 200m/650ft, followed by a descent of 1000m/3300ft; equipment and access as the main walk, return by 354 from Icod el Alto to Puerto (Timetable 4); journey time 35min. Use the map on pages 82-83 to find your way (Walk 14 in reverse).

2 El Lagar — La Vega: 15km/9.3mi; 4h10min; easy-moderate, with a descent of 500m/1650ft at the end and short ascent to La Vega; equipment and access/return as for main walk (but leave your taxi at El Lagar). Follow the main walk from the 3h-point.

3 La Guancha — El Lagar — La Guancha: 10km/6.2mi; 4h30min; moderate-strenuous ascent/descent of 600m/1950ft; equipment and access by bus as above; return on the same bus. See notes on page 88.

4 Campamento Barranco de la Arena — Canal Vergara — La Guancha: 11.5km/7.1mi; 4h25min; moderate ascent of 200m/650ft, followed by a descent of 1000m/3300ft; equipment and access as main walk; return on the same bus. Follow the main walk to the 3h-point, then pick up the notes for Walk 14 from the 7h40min-point (page 84) to return to La Guancha.

From the lovely camping and picnic area of Barranco de la Arena (also visited in Walk 14), this walk first climbs through picturesque pines and over rocky crests up to Galería Vergara Alta at 1500m/4925ft. On the way you'll pass its younger brother, Galería Vergara Baja. Vergara Alta and the *canal* it feeds are responsible for a large supply of water conveyed to the southern side of the island; it has been operating since the early 1950s. This gallery goes back some 3.5 kilometres (over two miles) into the mountainside, and they're still excavating!

Leave your taxi at the campsite and **start out** by locating a covered concrete watercourse running roughly north/south, above the track. Follow it uphill for some metres/yards, keeping it on your right. A clear path (lined with stones) soon shows itself, which you follow uphill. Meet a forestry track about 10 minutes up, and follow it to the right. You pass Galería Vergara Baja in

about **25min**. Less than 10 minutes past this *galería*, just beyond the second bend in the track, take the small path on your left. Five minutes up you meet the track again. Keep alongside the fairly large pipe on the left and, on a curve, re-enter the heather, with the pipe. On rejoining the track, on the same bend, scramble up a low embankment and continue on the path. Re-meet the track, and find your path 30m/yds up, heading back into vegetation. At **50min** Canal Vergara is a minute up, just off the track, to the right. You won't see it until you are halfway there. A small concrete tank marks it. The *canal* splits here for La Guancha and the south. (You will notice that signs prohibit walking atop the *canal*, to avoid damage to the concrete surface.) Continue uphill to Galería Vergara Alta (**1h**).

From here return the same way to the campsite (**1h45min**) and, from there, follow the track to El Lagar. (This route is described in Walk 14: pick up those notes and map from the 6h25min-point, pages 82-83.)

From El Lagar (**3h**; sketch map pages 88-89) take the track in front of the forestry house and head west. Stay on this track for **two and a half hours**, ignoring all junctions and turn-offs. The dense pine forest allows hardly any views, but the scent from the trees and the earthen path is a tonic. The walk remains on more or less the same contour (at about 1100m/3600ft) all the way to the Las Abiertas turn-off (**5h30min**).

Here go right (a left turn leads to San José de los

Llanos). Five minutes downhill, ignore a fork off to the right. The route alternates between concrete and gravel. Some 20 minutes from the junction meet a road and continue straight downhill. About 20 minutes later meet a road coming in from the right and, a minute downhill, swing left along it. This brings you down to the La Montañeta/Icod road (**6h40min**). You could catch a bus here, but head up left into La Vega. You reach a first bar, on your left, in **7h10min**. The bus stops at the intersection here, opposite a small supermarket.

Alternative walk 15-3: from La Guancha to El Lagar (and Campamento Barranco de la Arena); *refer to map pages 82-83*

The bus from Puerto stops not far past the service station (on the right) in La Guancha. Once off the bus, cross the road. Some 200m/yds uphill you will see steps flanked by troughs of bright geraniums. **Start out here**: climb these steps. Keep right at the top of them and head uphill. In five minutes, bear right again. A few minutes up this road will find you below a games court. Take the drive up to it. The path begins here, to the right of the court. Follow it uphill until you come onto a concrete drive. Turn left, walk up the drive and, when it swings left, bear right on a path. Go straight up this path (don't turn off to the right). Ignore the small path off left a minute later; keep right. Twenty minutes later, take a small path off right. In a minute it joins a disused track. Once again, turn right, and follow this track to the tarred road. Cross it, and continue straight on up the cobbled track. Your track continues straight on *over* the forestry track (now no longer tarred). When you next cross the track, head up slightly left, through young pines. Some 20 minutes later cross again: your way, now a path, continues opposite. As you begin this gentle climb, keep right. Over 10 minutes later, leave this path at a junction: go right and, a few metres/yards uphill, on the left, your path continues again

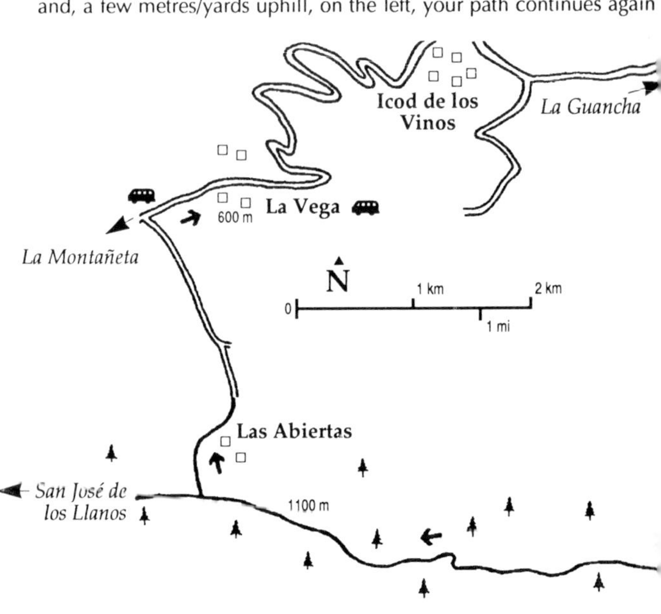

Woodcutters' paths lead through a magnificent pine forest, on the approach El Lagar (Picnic 14, Alternative walk 15-3).

(if it is overgrown, keep to the track). In 10 minutes, recross the forestry track on a bend: your path lies opposite. At the next crossing, your path is slightly right. Ten minutes later, cross the track for the last time: to reach your path, scramble up the low embankment. On coming to a fork in the path a minute up, keep left and then straight up the spine of the ridge. When you come out onto the track again, follow it to the right to El Lagar (2h30min), where there is a forestry house, as well as a large *zona recreativa*.

To continue to Barranco de la Arena, head up to the left of the forestry house. Four minutes will bring you to a culvert crossing. Just before the culvert, on the right, there's a small path running alongside a narrow water pipe. Follow this path which dips and then immediately swings left up an embankment. Cross over a flat area, to a low-lying rocky ridge, where you pick up the continuation of your path. You rejoin the pipe further up as you climb a ridge with sweeping views across undulating crests of pines. Your route twists between large boulders; for part of the way, you're above the track. Keep the water pipe in sight as you continue straight up. Minutes later come out onto a forestry track. Rejoin your path half a minute up, on the right, on a bend in the track (just beyond a small mound). You remeet the forestry track: don't turn right immediately; keep straight ahead, go through a barrier and into Campamento Barranco de la Arena (4h25min). Return the same way.

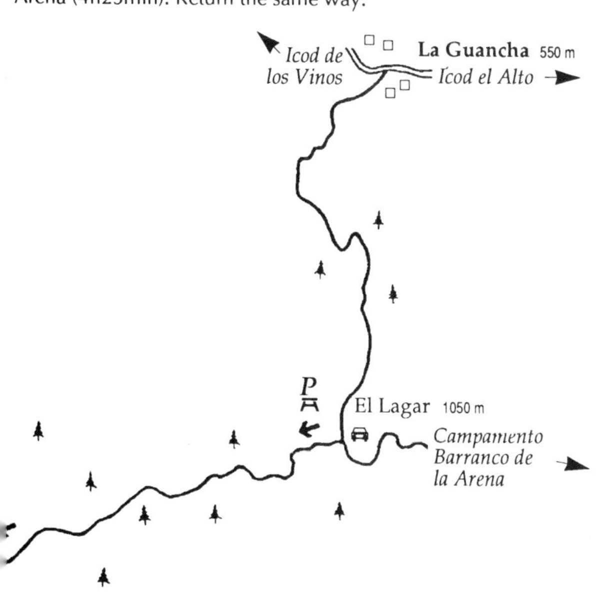

16 LA MONTAÑETA • LAS ARENAS NEGRAS • LOS PARTIDOS DE TRANQUIS • C820

See also photograph page 93

Distance: 10.5km/6.5mi; 4h10min

Grade: fairly easy, with an ascent of 300m/1000ft at the start and a descent of 300m/1000ft at the end

Equipment: stout shoes, sunhat, cardigan, anorak, raingear, picnic, water

How to get there: 🚌 363 from Puerto to Icod de los Vinos (Timetable 6); journey time 45min; *change to* 🚌 360 to La Montañeta (Timetable 8); journey time 35min
To return: 🚌 460 from the San José de los Llanos turn-off on the C820 to Icod de los Vinos (Timetable 7); journey time 40min; *change to* 🚌 363 from Icod to Puerto (Timetable 6); journey time 45min

For length and variety, this walk is one of my favourites. A short climb up through pines brings you to Las Arenas Negras, a picnic spot/recreation zone. On your way up you pass Montaña Negra, a large black mound of sand. The real impact of this short stretch of intriguing beauty comes as you meander round the smooth undulating landscape: all the other colours are accentuated by the backdrop of black sand. Once out of the pines, you're all alone, passing through wild, open country, high above a plain. It is across this plain that you continue to your bus stop, via the hamlet of Los Partidos de Tranquis.

The walk starts on the path behind the 'Respete la Naturaleza' sign, just uphill from the bus stop and across the road from a chapel. Climb the crest directly behind the sign. In five minutes meet an old track: turn left uphill. You cross the Los Llanos road in **10min** and the forestry track to Las Arenas Negras five minutes later. Ignore a turn-off left three minutes later. At **25min** come out of the trees and meet a junction: go straight ahead uphill (the right-hand fork). Having ignored a faint fork off to the left, you reach Las Arenas Negras (Picnic 16) at the **1h**-mark.

Continue up the track for another 25 minutes, to find

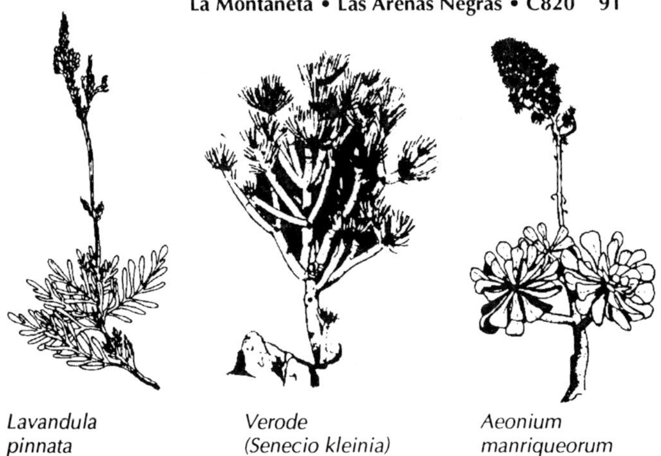

Lavandula pinnata

Verode (Senecio kleinia)

Aeonium manriqueorum

yourself in the alluring confines of Montaña Negra. This stark, enclosed landscape comes ablaze as the sand shimmers and the encircling pines flicker under the bright sun. Soon you see two concrete buildings ahead: they are perched on one of the island's longest and most important watercourses, the Canal Vergara (see notes at the start of Walk 15, page 86). Fork right on the track just below the *canal* (walking atop the watercourse, as indicated by the green line on the map, is no longer permitted). You head back towards the volcanic fields of black sand (**2h 15min**).

After 15 minutes' strolling, you'll find the trees thinning out and the sands opening up before you. Clusters of sharp grey rock attract your attention with

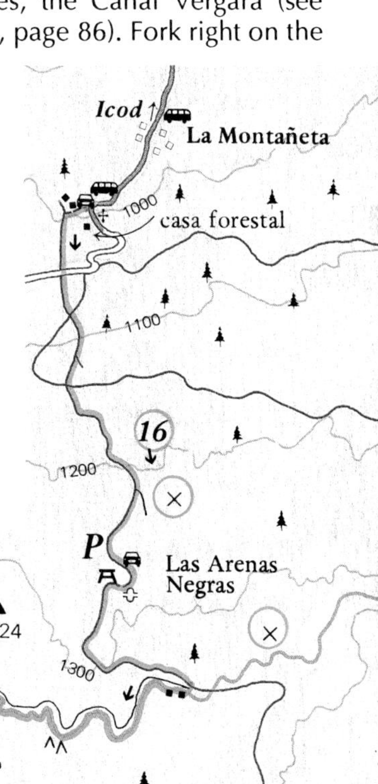

Las Arenas Negras (Picnic 16; Car tour 3)

their patchy coating of thick rusty-orange lichen. Baby pine trees, planted out symmetrically in a hollow immediately in front of you, catch your eye. Montaña Negra is now beside you on the right. On passing it, you'll see a long rough tail of crusted lava heading seaward. Just past Montaña Negra you reach the ascending point for the peak. *Be warned* — this is a jeep safari stop. The optional ascent (not included in the times) takes under 10 minutes and offers a stupendous panorama, with especially good views of El Teide.

You briefly re-enter the pines. Soon a magnificent viewpoint greets you. On a clear day, La Gomera can be seen clearly — even its villages! To the right lie the twin humps of La Palma. Los Llanos betrays its secluded location on the far right. About an hour along this track, come to a junction of four tracks (**3h15min**) and turn right. Keep downhill, ignoring the many turn-offs. About 10 minutes down, you're in a basin, and the track veers left to make its way across the plain. Having descended below 1200m, at **3h40min**, meet a junction and keep straight ahead (slightly left) on the main track.

The hamlet of Los Partidos de Tranquis marks the **3h45min**-point in the hike. It's situated in a very enviable location, sheltered from the winds and with El Teide as a backdrop. As you leave the basin, more signs of cultivation greet you. Beyond the hamlet, the road to San José de los Llanos cuts across your track. Turn left and follow it to the main Icod road (C820; **4h10min**). The lone bar/restaurant, set back in a quarried hillock about 50m/ yds downhill (right), is where you will catch your bus — or walk on to Erjos, some 20 minutes away.

17 ERJOS • PORTELA ALTA • EL PALMAR

Distance: 10.5km/6.5mi; 3h **See also photograph page 26**

Grade: fairly easy descent of 500m/1650ft on tracks

Equipment: stout shoes, sunhat, cardigan, anorak, water, picnic

How to get there: 🚌 363 from Puerto to Icod de los Vinos (Timetable 6); journey time 45min; *change to* 🚌 460 to Erjos (Timetable 7; journey time 35min)

To return: 🚌 366 from Portela Alta to Buenavista (Timetable 11); journey time 20min; *change to* 🚌 363 for Icod (Timetable 6); journey time 1h; *change to* connecting 🚌 363 for Puerto (Timetable 6); journey time 45min

Short walk: Erjos — viewpoint reached at 55min — Erjos: 8km/5mi; 1h45min; easy descent/ascent of 100m/330ft; access as above; return on the same bus.

Alternative walk: Erjos — El Palmar — Buenavista: 14km/8.7mi; 4h; fairly easy descent of 900m/2950ft on tracks. Access as above; return on 🚌 363 to Puerto (Timetable 6); journey time 45min. Follow the main walk for 3h. Then, where the street through El Palmar meets the main road (TF1426/7) keep straight downhill; don't join the main road. Short-cut paths and tracks (see map page 94) will take you straight down to Buenavista and the bus station in just over an hour.

This is a pleasant, easy stroll, through a relic of the tertiary period — the great laurel forest which covered southern Europe and North Africa some 15 million years ago. Today these flora are virtually extinct, but the Canarian archipelago harbours a few of the remaining sanctuaries. This evergreen forest is the result of climatic conditions brought about by the trade winds. At least ten species of laurel flourish here; the forest is also a refuge for ferns, fungi and lichen.

The bus ride itself brightens your day: the first thing to hit you will be the splendour of the colours — bright red poinsettias, blue morning glory, white, pink and red

Erjos: beyond the village rises a ridge, terraced from head to toe.

red oleander, and the ever-present bougainvillea, with its rich hues of scarlet, orange and purple. Canary date palms give the road a touch of elegance. You'll pass through picturesque San Juán de la Rambla and then come into the pleasant sprawling town of Icod de los Vinos (known for the dragon tree shown on page 25 and its local wines). The ongoing bus to Erjos climbs 800m/ 2600ft and affords some of the most splendid panoramas on the island. Rich pockets of volcanic soil are intensively tilled up this steep escarpment. The landscape becomes more wild higher up, and untamed greens blanket the countryside. Erjos is just a meek splash of white in this wilderness.

You'll be dropped off just past the church in Erjos, before the bus continues its journey to Guía de Isora. Follow

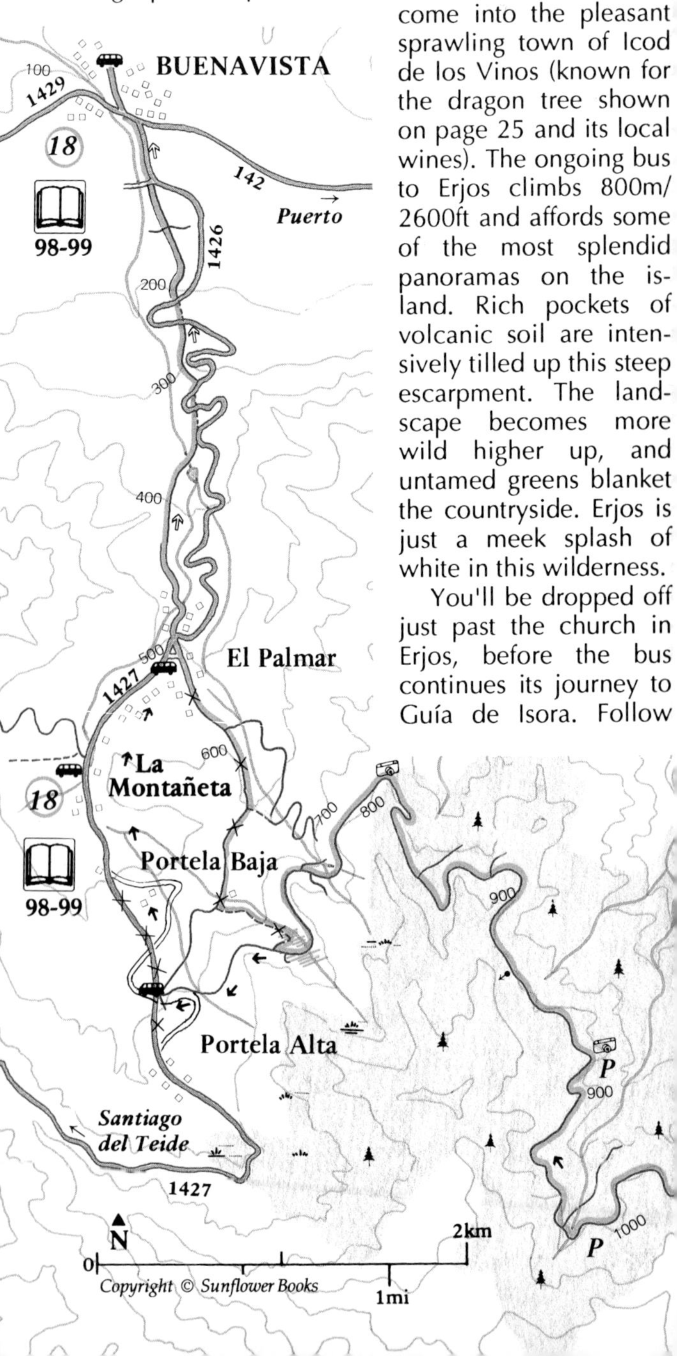

the main road uphill to the right for three minutes. A tall lone pine marks the spot where **the walk begins.** A forestry house lies across the road. Turn right: this forestry track will take you to Portela Alta. Keep left at a fork two minutes downhill, then ignore any branch-offs. You leave all sounds of civilisation behind, as the track disappears into an isolated valley of evergreens.

At **55min** you're rounding a wide bend and entering another part of the valley. Look back across the valley at the way you've just come. You will have caught glimpses of the coast through the trees, but soon it will come into full view. The vivid green of the banana palms can be seen through the conical peaks guarding the entrance to the valley. Small birds cross your way, and hawks glide in circles overhead. This is a lovely picnic spot (Picnic 17); *the Short walk turns back here.*

A refreshing drinking fountain makes a pleasant surprise at **1h20min**. Two minutes before entering the next valley (**1h30min**), on a curve, you get an uninterrupted view of Tierra del Trigo (the Land of Wheat), concealed on the valley's far inner slopes. It's the only sign of cultivation up here. As you cross a crest, the entrance to the El Palmar valley (photograph page 26), you'll be struck by the absence of trees: the entire basin is terraced, from top to bottom, right to left. El Palmar lies almost immediately below and, much further down on the plain, Buenavista sits surrounded by banana palms.

At **2h20min** you meet the TF1427 at Portela Alta. A bus shelter is 80m/yds downhill to the right. To reach El Palmar, follow the path behind the bus shelter; it circles to the right of the school. Minutes down, cross the road and follow a concrete drive. Again cross the road and continue on a tarred lane. Some 30 minutes from the bus stop you are walking parallel with the main road and entering El Palmar (**3h**). If you're not too tired, why not continue to Buenavista (Alternative walk), from where there are more frequent buses?

18 LA MONTAÑETA • TENO ALTO • TENO BAJO • (FARO DE TENO) • BUENAVISTA

Distance: 20km/12.5mi; 6h50min (add 1h for detour to lighthouse)

Grade: strenuous, with a total climb of 400m/1300ft and descent of 800m/2600ft. There is the additional hazard of loose stones on the final descent. **Possibility of vertigo** on two short-cut paths

Equipment: walking boots, sunhat, cardigan, anorak, picnic, plenty of water, swimwear; a torch is *essential* for the road tunnel

How to get there: 🚌 363 from Puerto to Buenavista (Timetable 6); journey time 1h45min; *change to* 🚌 366 to La Montañeta (Timetable 11); journey time 20min; ask for 'el camino para Teno Alto'. You could take a taxi for this short trip of 5km; ask for 'el camino para Teno Alto'.

To return: 🚌 363 from Buenavista to Puerto (Timetable 6); journey time 1h45min

Shorter walk: La Montañeta — Teno Alto — La Montañeta: 9km/5.6mi; 4h20min; strenuous; equipment as above, but stout shoes will suffice. Follow the main walk to Teno Alto. From the bar, turn right and follow the road (no turn-offs) for about 55min, when the road will begin to descend. Descend on the road for a further 15min, to re-reach the path you climbed from La Montañeta. Return to Buenavista on 🚌 366 (Timetable 11) or telephone for a taxi.

The high, hidden, segmented valleys of the Teno are a must for those with stamina. This isolated severe landscape has a stark beauty, with soft colours emanating from the earth itself. Solitude and peace immediately come to mind. The hardships that these few inhabitants have chosen to face leave one admiring, perhaps even envying, their fortitude.

Ask your taxi or bus driver for 'el camino para Teno Alto'. This road (*camino*) is barely half a kilometre past El Palmar (Walk 17), a sleepy conglomeration of houses. By bus, push the button as you pass the turn-off for Teno Alto. The stop is outside a building with a couple of shops. Head back to the signposted road to Teno Alto. **Your path begins** just inside this turn-off: it runs alongside the concrete-block wall on your left (where there is usually a sign for Los Viñatigos) and then up between sagging stone walls. A trellised vineyard is entrenched below.

When you have climbed to the road (**25min**), leave the path and follow the road for the next 90 minutes. You won't see any traffic, and your views command the entire valley. The entry point to the hidden valleys of Teno is the summit of a ridge, reached at **2h**. You won't be prepared for what you see on the other side — it's a completely different world. The bleakness and ruggedness begin to capture your imagination. You're at about 800m/2600ft here; the highest point of this great mass is

Montaña Baracán at 1003m/3290ft, not far away on the left. Soon the heights of Teno are seen.

Your turn-off is just beyond this viewpoint: three minutes along, you'll see a track forking off to the right. Your path is just beyond this track, and it forks off right between a cairn and a sign for San Jerónimo/Los Viñatigos. (Those prone to vertigo might feel uneasy along this short stretch.) Come to a grassy path at the bottom of a first small gulley; here bear right. At **2h15min** bear right along the crest and begin to descend into a second gulley. After climbing a neatly-paved section of path, round a bend and soon find yourself on a track by a small farm building. Follow this track for eight minutes, then take the wide cobbled path off to the right (just where the track swings left). You re-meet the Teno Alto road several minutes uphill, cross it and take the earthen path opposite you. Soon your curiosity will be satisfied. Teno Alto (Upper Teno) lies just over this ridge. Rejoin the road and head into the village (**2h55min**), *from where the Shorter walk turns back.*

On the dramatic descent to Teno Bajo

To make for Teno Bajo (Lower Teno), keep straight on. The road becomes a track, and you cross a slight crest and descend into another valley. Within 10 minutes you reach another crest and a junction, where there is a house on the right. Continue straight over the crest and then downhill, ignoring a track off to the right. At **3h15min** you round a bend and come to a T-junction. Your way is downhill, to the right. (From here you can follow the track until it ends, or take the short-cuts described below. If you follow the track, add 20 minutes.) A few minutes later, a farm track joins you from the left. Head left towards the ravine here. Then continue down along the edge of the ravine (another stretch which some people may find vertiginous). At **3h30min**, you come onto the track again, above a few buildings. Stay on the track until, 20m/yds below one of these buildings (a house on a bend, just before the track veers right), you can descend to the left. Follow the 2-inch water pipe. There is no real path, but the rock wall is on your right, and the ravine is to the left. Pass two old rock buildings several minutes down, and then another two. Some metres/yards before the last of the dwellings, fork left down a path.

You quickly reach the *barranco.* Down here you rejoin the track (**3h45min**). Keep left. As you leave the ravine, you pass a circular rock-tiled threshing floor. Along this part of the track, more of the coastal tongue comes into view, where dark lava shades meet the royal-blue sea. The track comes to a dead end at **4h**,

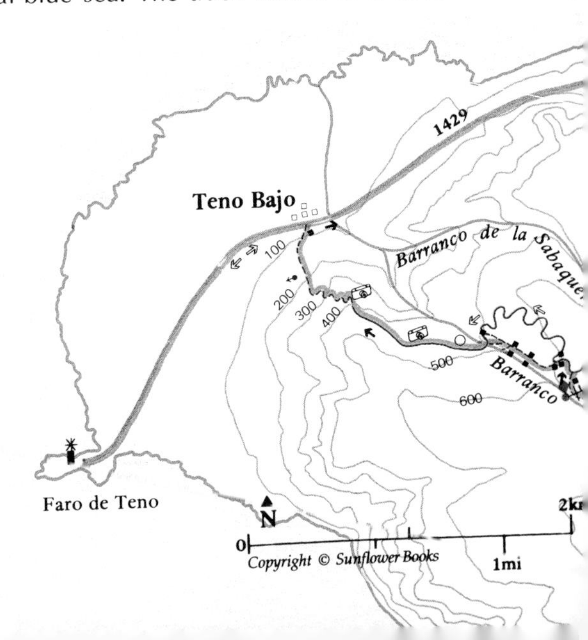

high above the plain. This is an excellent viewpoint: to your right, a jagged ravine cuts back into the mountainside; to the left is the subdued coastline's only landmark: the lighthouse, sitting on a promontory of black lava. Spread out below you are the green-patterned fields of a plantation. On clear days you see La Gomera — its mountains rise very clearly out of the sea, and the two humps of La Palma stand out over to the right.

At the end of the track there is a large boulder with a splash of white paint on it. Bear left just *before* reaching the boulder, and you'll pick up your path on the left. You zigzag down the sheer escarpment. Loose rocks and gravel make it very slow going, so enjoy the superb descent (photograph page 97) *in pauses, not while on the move!* Your only landmark on this stretch is a water tank, about 30 minutes downhill. At **4h50min** your path ends at the left of a large shed at Teno Bajo (from where it's an easy hour's stroll to the lighthouse and back).

From here follow the road (TF1429) eastwards, enjoying spectacular coastal scenery. A torch is *essential* for the tunnels. At **5h45min** pass by Punta del Fraile (Picnic 18), from where there are magnificent views out over the banana groves surrounding Buenavista, which is reached after **6h50min**.

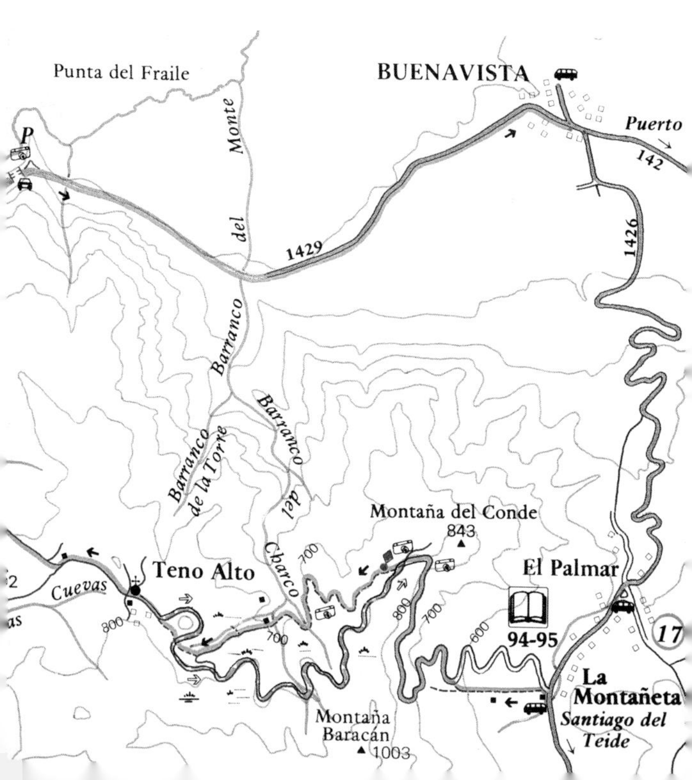

19 PUNTA DEL HIDALGO • CHINAMADA • LAS CARBONERAS

Map on reverse of the fold-out touring map; cover photograph

Distance: 7km/4.3mi; 4h

Grade: moderate-strenuous climb (700m/2300ft overall); **possibility of vertigo**

Equipment: stout shoes, cardigans, anorak, raingear, sunhat, picnic, water

How to get there: 🚌 102 from Puerto to La Laguna (Timetable 1); journey time 45min; *change to* 🚌 105 to Punta del Hidalgo (Timetable 13); journey time 40min

To return: 🚌 1.705 from Las Carboneras to La Laguna (Timetable 16); journey time 1h05min; *change to* 🚌 102 to Puerto (as above)

Alternative walk: Las Carboneras — Chinamada — Las Carboneras: 6km/3.7mi; 3h; easy-moderate, with ups and downs of about 300m/1000ft. Access as for Walk 20, page 103; return by the same bus. From the bus stop, walk back out of Las Carboneras for four minutes, past the last house (on a bend). Then take the path on the right, signposted to Las Escaleras. Immediately into the path, turn left. You'll come to the Escaleras *mirador,* at a junction, in 35min (Picnic 19b). Keep right at the junction. When the path forks, head uphill right. At an abandoned house, turn right and walk behind it, not downhill. A few minutes later, when the path forks, head downhill to the road at Chinamada and turn right for Las Carboneras.

Your starting point, Punta del Hidalgo, sits at the end of a steep ridge running down to the coast from the heights of the Anaga range. Get off the bus at the *mirador* just past the village, above the mouth of Barranco del Tomadero. The valley looks impassable from here, as it rises steeply into sharp-edged ridges. Playa de los Troches (Picnic 19a), a rocky beach, is partially hidden by the cliffs below. All this comes as an abrupt change from the market garden plains of La Laguna and the rolling meadows of Tegueste, a wide,

Chinamada: like the Guanches, many of these country folk have made their homes in caves nestled in the rocky faces of the ridge.

sloping valley passed on your descent to Punta del Hidalgo. Chinamada, a tiny, sprinkled hamlet, will delight you with its cave dwellings.

Start the walk at the *mirador*. Follow the concrete drive below the viewpoint down to the right (signposted for Chinamada and Las Carboneras). In a few minutes, with the beach falling away below you on your left, you pass a large greenhouse. The track surface changes to gravel. Continue straight downhill. Soon your track ends, just before a rocky promontory. Continue down a concrete drive behind a chain barrier, descending steeply into the *barranco*. The twin peaks of Los Hermanos (The Brothers; see cover photograph) rise up ahead. Typical coastal, salt-resistant vegetation accompanies you: *tabaiba, verode* and *Aeoniums*. The drive brings you to a building and a log bridge crossing the mouth of the Barranco del Tomadero (**10min**). This is a beautiful quiet spot. Once over the stream, you begin ascending this *barranco* on a path cut into the embankment (a minute up pass a sign for Chinamada).

Above the *barranco* you skirt a thick stone wall. As you begin your (sometimes vertiginous) ascent, great arms of *cardón,* growing out of the slope, will leave you astonished at their size. Purple flowers enrich the setting, too — especially the sea lavender which begins flowering in January. Caves of varying sizes and shapes scar the ridge. At about **1h40min** into the walk, come to a look-out point with superb views towards sharp, abrupt ridges dropping down to the sea. From here, bright yellow flowers line the path as you head uphill. More fine views follow as the path briefly makes its way along the edge of the cliffs, where you will hear and see birds darting about. Then, once again, you head back into the valley. In some places steps have been carved into the rocky surface to help you gain height.

Soon you will notice a distinct change in the vegetation. *Asphodelus,* with its long, thin green leaves and flowers, covers the slope, with the help of grass. A few terraced plots dig back into the inclines. A grassy hill, hanging off the top of a ridge, marks a good spot for surveying the valley below and the banana palms engulfing Punta del Hidalgo. From here on, the way becomes steeper, with more steps cut into the edge of the ridge.

A kingdom of sheer, narrow valleys segments the range. Farmers have terraced the slightest ease in the mountainsides, from the summits down. On rounding a bend (**3h10min**), neat stepped plots announce the beginnings of Chinamada. You'll probably reach for your camera at once, to capture on film the houses snuggled into the mountainside. Stone-terraced gardens sit below them. Just past the dwellings you meet a wide gravel road and pass a chapel. Follow this road all the way to Las Carboneras. Beyond the chapel fresh meadows, full of clover, roll off the slopes. The mountaintops in front of you are now covered in trees and heather. After passing a dragon tree on your left (photograph page 100), come to a lovely little white house protruding out of a stone wall. A minute uphill, another house lies over to your right. The driveway off to the right by this latter house (**3h20min**) is descended in the *Alternative walk.* Don't forget to look back as you go along — there's another of these amazing little cave dwellings, even more remote than the others, over to your left.

The road cuts through a ridge. One of your lasting memories of this walk is likely to be the continuous bleating of goats ringing out across the valley. Pass below the trees and soon a spectacular view hits you at the **3h40min**-mark, as you cross another crest. A deep, long valley runs horizontally far below. A finely-etched ridge rises up from this valley, leaving only the highest elevations of the Anaga in view. The Roque de Taborno sits raised above the rest of the razor-sharp crest. Taborno itself, a few white dwellings, straddles this ridge midway. What an enviable view the small farmhouse on your left (Picnic 19c) must have!

Las Carboneras is now only 20 minutes away: head right. When you reach the village, you'll be charmed by the attractive mixture of old and new houses, resting on a cultivated hillock extending into the valley. The bus stop is at the village entrance, by the church (**4h**).

Taborno, dominated by its rock — the 'Little Matterhorn' (Walk 20, Picnic 20, Car tour 4)

20 LAS CARBONERAS • TABORNO • ROQUE DE TABORNO • CASA NEGRIN

Map on reverse of fold-out touring map; see also photograph opposite

Distance: 8km/5mi; 4h25min

Grade: strenuous, with ascents totalling about 600m/2000ft; *the main walk is recommended for experts only* (see also Alternative walk); **danger of vertigo** at the Roque de Taborno.

Equipment: walking boots, cardigans, anorak, raingear, sunhat, whistle, water, picnic (but see notes about a restaurant in the text)

How to get there: 🚌 102 from Puerto to La Laguna (Timetable 1); journey time 45min; *change to* 🚌 1.705 to Las Carboneras (Timetable 16); journey time 40 minutes
To return: same buses

Alternative walk: Las Carboneras — base of Roque de Taborno — Las Carboneras: 7km/4.3mi; 2h30min; grade as above, but without the vertiginous and potentially dangerous circuit of the rock. Access/return as above. Follow the main walk for 1h40min, then return to the 1h30min-point in the walk. From there pick up the main walk again at the 2h20min-mark to reach Casa Negrín.

You enjoy a first view of Roque de Taborno when the bus emerges from the wooded slopes on its descent to Las Carboneras. This perfectly-shaped 'spike' (see opposite) is a prominent feature of the Anaga's landscape of razor-sharp crests. Your hike circles the base of this great sculpture. From the north side of the rock, a wealth of coastal scenery lies before you. The small pockets of fertile, stepped slopes sitting far out of reach give you some idea of the value of arable land. If you haven't brought a picnic, Casa Negrín, the little *restaurante típico* at the end of the walk, will add to your enjoyment. Crowded with local workmen and businessmen alike, it's a real 'find'. Good news — the bus comes to you! It stops at the turn-off a few minutes west of the restaurant (which is also called 'Casa Carlos' and is *closed Wednesdays*). So eat, drink, and be merry!

Start out at the bus stop in Las Carboneras. Head back out of the village, the way the bus came, for 150m/yds. When you are opposite the Bar Valentin, leave the road, taking the path heading down into the *barranco* on your left. This clear path takes you down grassy slopes, past plots. At a fork five minutes down, keep right. Under 10 minutes beyond a second electricity pylon, two streams cross your path and soon become one. Just after, pass a fork off to the right, and five minutes later continue straight ahead (ignore the branch-off to the left). Always remain on the widest path, since many paths branch off to plots. In a further five minutes (beyond a wicker gate on the right), cross

The Anaga Peninsula, from Casa Negrín (Picnic 21; Walks 20, 21; Car tours 2 and 4)

the stream in the Barranco de Taborno. Now, on your very steep ascent up the other side, ignore any side-paths. Fifteen minutes up from the *barranco,* keep left at a fork. At **1h** you should reach the TF1128; turn left to Taborno (**1h10min**). The village square is strategically placed atop the high, thin ridge partitioning the Barranco de Taborno and the Barranco Afur de Tamadite. This widely-dispersed village could undoubtedly claim to have the best views on the entire island.

Facing the small chapel in the square, head up the steps at the right of it. A couple of minutes up, veer right. Three minutes along, when the path forks, bear right (don't go up the steps). All the houses here are tiny and well-glued to the top of the ridge. Little gardens hug their bases, and prickly pear and aloes surround the lot. Follow the path until, at the bottom of some steps, it forks. Here, turn left downhill, through a small open copse. At the next fork swing right just past a narrow ridge of rock. Head towards a small house and pass above it (**1h30min**). On rounding the nose of a ridge, you enjoy superb views (Picnic 20): Playa del Tamadite is seen at the mouth of the *barranco* far below on your right, and the two Roques de Anaga sit off the shore.

Soon the ridge narrows, and you continue along the crest. The walls of the Barranco de Taborno are quite spectacular from here. Dykes, emerging out of the rock face, give the walls veins. Horizontal strips of smooth green mark the patches of cultivation along the slopes of the ridge. Three minutes along this neck of land, your path forks. Head left uphill. On reaching the summit, turn right and continue around the side of the slope.

A small stone hut/goat pen, built into the rock on the crest above you, is reached several minutes later (**1h 40min**). You are now near the base of the rock, which looks less impressive from this angle. *The Alternative walk turns back here.* To begin circling the rock, head down to the left. No turn-offs are necessary, so ignore the path off left in five minutes — it only goes to a goats' pen. After about ten minutes' walking round the rock, just past a pile of rocks and round the end of a small ridge, the route changes abruptly. Don't continue past the plots in front of you: climb steeply up the ridge just to your right. Your target is the rock: head up to it, over rocks and along goats' paths. On nearing the rock, continue round to the left (those who suffer from vertigo may find this stretch unnerving). Ahead, razor-sharp peaks along the coastline fall into the sea, and Almáciga (Walk 24; photograph page 18) is a cluster of white, lost in the upheaval of pinnacles to the east.

At **2h** you will find yourself just below the peak of Roque de Taborno. The beautiful Afur Valley opens up. Half a minute later, come to a halt: it seems that there is nowhere to go! A goats' pen, securely set in the side of the rock, sits just in front of you, and the side of the ridge drops away in every other direction. Head *through* the pen and leave by its gate. You think you will drop off into space, but closer inspection reveals a narrow path clinging to the rock. *Cautiously* make your way round the side of the rock; this vertiginous stretch takes about half a minute. This goats' path leads you back to the first goats' pen you passed, but now *above* it. Clamber down to it and back downhill to your original path. Retrace your steps to the house first met at 1h30min into the walk (**2h20min**). Just past this house, climb down the right-hand side of the ridge and join a path below you. Now you are in the higher elevations of a precipitous, winding ravine, the Barranco de Taborno. Always keep left and uphill. You regain the centre of Taborno at **2h35min**.

Leaving Taborno (just past the last house), take the steps on your left, signposted 'Casa Negrín'. This path leads you up to the crest of the ridge you've been walking. Stay on the top of this ridge *(always keeping to the widest, clearest path)* and huff and puff your way up to Casa Negrín (**4h25min**). The bus stop is two minutes along the road (go right at the junction).

21 CASA NEGRIN • AFUR • PLAYA DEL TAMADITE • AFUR • ROQUE NEGRO

Map on reverse of the fold-out touring map; see also photographs pages 104, 113

Distance: 12.5km/7.8mi; 6h40min

Grade: very strenuous descent of 900m/3000ft and ascent of 800m/2600ft; **possibility of vertigo**; *recommended for experts only*

Equipment: walking boots, cardigans, anorak, sunhat, raingear, whistle, picnic, water

How to get there: 🚌 102 from Puerto to La Laguna (Timetable 1); journey time 45min; *change to* 🚌 1.705 to Casa Negrín (Timetable 16); journey time 25min

To return: 🚌 1.706 from Roque Negro to La Laguna (Timetable 17); journey time about 1h05min, or 🚌 1.710 from the Roque Negro turn-off to La Laguna (Timetable 18); journey time 45min; *change to* 🚌 102 to Puerto (as above)

Short walk: Casa Negrín — Taborno — Casa Negrín: 7km/4.3mi; 3h10min; moderate descent/ascent of 400m/1300ft. Access as above; return on the same bus. Follow the main walk for 50min. Instead of going right, head left and follow the track to Taborno. Then pick up Walk 20 at the 2h35min-point (page 105), to get back to Casa Negrín.

Winter is often wet, but the Afur valley is at its best then. The main stream almost becomes a river, and the pools are big enough to swim in. Summer reduces the stream to a weary trickle, with only a few

A precariously-perched cave dwelling, en route from Afur to Roque Negro

pools remaining. The days are hot then, and the landscape burns under the strong sun as the fresh green flora fade. The views on your descent open up the dim corners of this rugged landscape, and the sound of cascading water accompanies you for much of the way. Your ascent — tough as it is — is made easier by a couple of local bars, full of atmosphere!

Casa Negrín (or 'Casa Carlos'; see photograph page 104) is just downhill from where you leave the bus. **Start out here**: take the track running downhill, on the right-hand side of the restaurant. A minute down, pass to the left of another house. Here, the track becomes a wide path (*very slippery when wet*), as it slides down the ridge. In less than five minutes you meet a junction: continue straight downhill. A minute later, find yourself above a small weekend cottage secured to the top of the ridge, overlooking the Afur Valley (Picnic 21).

At **25min** you pass through another intersection: keep straight on, along the widest path. Two minutes later, you leave this ridge and descend a path on your right (there is a telephone pole just past this turn-off). You zigzag down onto an adjoining ridge. The way evens out five minutes downhill, and you're looking into the Barranco de Guardoz. Your route continues along the crest of the ridge, with uninterrupted vistas of Taborno and Roque Negro, the black, monumental mound of rock rising up out of the landscape on your right. A small white village of the same name nestles slightly below it. A junction soon comes up: continue straight ahead along the top of the ridge.

You meet the Taborno track at **50min**. *The Short walk bears left here.* Cross the track and, just below it, come to a water tap. Two houses stand on your left, and a stupendous panorama lies before you: Playa del Tamadite (your next landfall), the far ridges that rise and fall as they head seaward, and Roque Negro. From the water tap, continue down over the ridge on your right, keeping left at a fork. As you descend, hamlets and solitary houses appear out of nowhere, on all sides of the valley. Two minutes down, you pass beside three cave dwellings built into the rocky escarpment. The path brushes to the left of them and falls away to the valley floor. Two paths join you from the right within the next ten minutes. Soon a most beautiful sight awaits you — an intimate cluster of white cottages, hedged in behind prickly pear, cuddling a crest of rock. You pass just below this hamlet and then swing over to the left side of the ridge and continue on down to the stream. Afur, lodged in a swollen ridge of rock, is seen at its best from this approach.

A bridge carries you across the stream at **1h25min**. After another crossing, a minute later, you climb to Afur (photograph page 113), where you'll find a bar just past the chapel. To make for the beach, follow the concrete path past the bar for for some 15m/yds, then turn right down an earthen path that passes to the right of the school. In two minutes join a path coming from the left and continue along it to your right. Almost at once come to a finger of rock standing alongside the path, on your left. You begin descending and find yourself not far above the stream and small cultivated plots.

At **1h40min**, at the end of a ridge, you leave the path and turn right. A large, balancing rock marks the spot. Once over the ridge, you pick up another path running inside the *barranco.* Two minutes along, you must descend a steep gravel rock face. A short piece of handrail is of some assistance on this *very hair-raising* stretch, and reassuring to those who suffer from vertigo. Just after **1h45min** you find yourself atop a crest. A steep descent takes you down across the stream. A dyke, slicing across the landscape and the *barranco,* brings you to a scenic spot in the gorge just after the stream crossing. Once across it, steps take you part of the way up the rocky embankment.

The beach comes into view at **2h05min**. On passing through a neat terraced vineyard two minutes further downhill, keep right and downhill. Your path is always safely above the stream, which flows in and out of narrow passages of rock. After six minutes of this descent, cross the stream and, just after it turns, cross it again, to regain the left-hand side. From here on, it's a matter making your own way, zigzagging across the stream. The beach is no more than 15 minutes away. En route you pass a couple of beautiful rock pools. Playa del Tamadite (**2h30min**) is a rocky beach flanked by sheer high cliffs. It's an ideal spot for solitude and swimming (but only in the freshwater pools — not in the sea, which is far too rough and dangerous).

After a relaxing picnic/swimming break, prepare yourself for the tiring return journey. Head back alongside the stream. Around 25 minutes uphill, you rejoin your path (after crossing the stream twice, just on a bend). The dyke, much more impressive from this approach, comes up at twenty-five minutes. *The descent down to it requires your full attention!*

You'll find yourself back in Afur in 1h30min (**4h**). The route to Roque Negro begins just behind the tall electricity building, past the chapel on the right. Five minutes will bring you to a bridge and the stream crossing. After crossing, turn left immediately and continue up to the houses above you. About 10 minutes from the village centre you pass an abandoned house. It's a gem, built into a large rock, out of which its two doors open. You leave this path some 10 minutes beyond the bridge, just as the way swings sharply right to a house. Here you turn left, then, almost immediately, swing back right again (just past a small house on the left). The path zigzags up the hillside. Don't take the path that cuts across immediately above the house. Your path is a minute uphill; it aims towards a television mast. This path leads you up above the two houses you've just passed and around the slope, into yet another *barranco*. A noticeable ascent begins just about where you come to a branch-off to the right. Ignore the branch-off and keep left all the way up. In 10 minutes, find yourself on top of a ridge, looking straight onto a sheer face of rock hanging onto the end of the ridge you are on. A little white cave dwelling sitting precariously on a thin ledge here makes quite a picture (photograph page 106). Two steps out of the front door, and you'd tumble into the gorge. From this point, head up to your right. Keep an eye open for the cave dwellings on the slopes to the right of Afur. Another path joins you from the left about 10 minutes past the house, and a second one comes from the right a few minutes later.

You meet the TF1127 some 50 minutes up from Afur (**4h50min**). You could catch the Roque Negro bus just here. The enormous 'Black Rock' for which the village is named surges up before you. Walk on into Roque Negro, then continue up the road for 12 minutes. Just after rounding a sharp bend, opposite a sign denoting the village of Roque Negro, climb the path on your left (signposted 'Degollada de las Hijas'). This wide path will take you to the main La Laguna road (TF1123) in another 1h50min (**6h40min**). The bus stops just where the path joins the road. Across the road you can enjoy superb views over both the northern and southern slopes of the Anaga, from the café.

22 PICO DEL INGLES • BARRANCO DE TAHODIO • SANTA CRUZ

Map on reverse of the fold-out touring map

Distance: 8km/5mi; 3h

Grade: easy-moderate descent of 1000m/3300ft

Equipment: stout shoes or walking boots, cardigan, anorak, sunhat, picnic, water

How to get there: 🚌 102 from Puerto to La Laguna (Timetable 1); journey time 45min; *change to* 🚌 1.705, 1.706, 1.708 or 1.710 (Timetables 16-19); journey time 30min. Ask for 'Pico del Inglés'; the bus stops at the turn-off to this viewpoint.
To return: 🚌 102 from Santa Cruz to Puerto (as above)

Mirador Pico del Inglés is the magnificent starting point for this walk. From this *mirador* you look out east to the mass of valleys cutting up the Punta de Anaga, and west to El Teide and the plains of La Laguna and La Esperanza. You also have a preview of your route immediately below on the right. The best time of year to do this walk is in winter, when small waterfalls and rock pools fill the bed of the Tahodio *barranco;* in summer the lower reaches are dry.

From the bus stop, head straight up to the *mirador* — some 10 minutes from the road. When you have enjoyed the views from the bar/restaurant (now closed), look for your sign, 'Barrio de la Alegría'. You'll find it just down the steps from the restaurant. **Start the walk here**: the path is flanked by tree heather; it takes you round the back of the building. Paths join you from the left three minutes and six minutes downhill; ignore them.

The old cobbled trail to the Barranco de la Alegría was once a very important route to Santa Cruz.

Come to the remains of a house and a cave (**15min**). A minute later, ignore a small path to the left. At under **20min** pass through an intersection, where there is another sign for Barrio de la Alegría. From the top of a crest you have views down into the valleys on either side (Picnic 22). The Barranco de Tahodio, on the right, has more character: ridges criss-cross its slopes, and dykes clearly mark the escarpment. A dark, muddy dam can be seen in the valley floor. At the **25min**-mark, when the path forks, keep right. As you descend, parts of Santa Cruz appear and, beyond it, the inclines of La Esperanza. El Teide, the island's masterpiece, rises impressively in the background. At about **45min** ignore two paths off to the left; bear right, in five minutes passing some abandoned dwellings high on the slopes. (You may notice two rooms cut into the side of the embankment, before you reach the houses.) Beyond another fork to the right, dogs warn you as you approach another abandoned house. When the path forks at just over **1h**, head right and soon come down to this house. Take the lower path that passes below it. Another sign for Barrio de la Alegría, just past the house, points you to the right.

Close on **1h20min** you cross the stream flowing down the narrow *barranco* floor. Pass below two more deserted houses a minute later. *Tabaiba* abounds here. Soon you are following the stream; if it has rained recently, there will be rock pools here. A small dam is seen across the stream at **1h30min**. A *canal,* fed by the dam, veers off around the slope on your right. Just past the dam, ignore the path to the right: keep left and head through abandoned fields. You re-cross the main stream at **1h40min** and again a few minutes later. Depending on the rainfall, you may find a small waterfall here. Some neat plots lie on your right, a few minutes later: almond, fig and loquat trees make this a pleasant spot. One more stream crossing brings you past a farm shed brightly ringed with geraniums. The *barranco* has narrowed quite considerably.

Cross the streambed twice more, and then meet a road at **2h15min**. Now follow the road for a tiring 3km/2mi; it takes you to Barrio de la Alegría, another 45 minutes down the *barranco* (**3h**). This suburb of Santa Cruz is stepped up the hillside. Catch a bus on the main road; a stop is on the right, not far below the junction.

23 TAGANANA • AFUR • TABORNO • LAS CARBONERAS

Map on reverse of touring map; see also photograph page 102

Distance: 9.2km/5.7mi; 5h10min

Grade: strenuous, with steep ascents (900m/3000ft overall) and descents (500m/1650ft overall)

Equipment: walking boots, sunhat, cardigans, anorak, raingear, water, picnic

How to get there: 🚌 102 from Puerto to Santa Cruz (Timetable 1); journey time 1h; *change to* 🚌 246 to Taganana (Timetable 14); journey time 45min

To return: 🚌 1.705 from Las Carboneras to La Laguna (Timetable 16); journey time 1h05min; *change* to 🚌 102 to Puerto (as above)

Short walk: Taganana — viewpoint over the Afur and Taganana valleys — Taganana: 4.5km/2.8mi; 3h; moderate ascent/descent of under 400m/1300ft; equipment as above, but stout shoes will suffice. Follow the main walk for 2h and return the same way to catch 🚌 246 (Timetable 14) to Santa Cruz.

Discovering the rural depths of the Anaga involves high ascents over long lateral ridges, and descents into deep, shady valleys. Farmers will be working the land, laden donkeys will pass you by, women — if they are not working in the fields — will be doing the washing, and children will be echoing across the valleys as they bound up the slopes. While this walk is strenuous it is not terribly *long,* and since there is a late return bus, you can take it at a leisurely pace.

Taganana is a beautiful farming village with cobbled streets and typical Canarian dwellings. Before you enter the village, a large ICONA signpost, on the right, alerts you to your bus stop. The bus shelter, where **the walk starts**, is in a parking bay. Cross the road and follow the narrow tarred road up into the village. Within a minute reach a junction. Here turn left and then immediately right. In half a minute, you come to another junction turn left. Here's your chance to capture some really good photos of rural life: arms of closely-knit houses extend down and across the slope. Palms, loquats dragon trees and orange trees adorn individual gardens.

On passing over a small bridge, the road heads up the slope, but you do not. Beyond the bridge (**5min**) turn left up a narrow street which soon becomes a wide cobbled path. A few minutes of winding up between beautiful old houses brings you onto the road again where you bear left. The last houses in the village huddle along the sides of a *barranco.* Where the road continues to the left, take the path that skirts the right hand side of this gulley (behind a sign which indicate no entry except for motorbikes). Beyond some houses, 50m/yds up on your left, a cosy white dwelling snuggles in amongst green trees and bushes, with dashes of colour from blooms — another perfect village scene.

At about **50min**, at a fork, go right for Afur (Picnic 23). You pass freshly-tilled land, where farmers will be hard at work. Higher up on the grassy slopes, shepherds saunter along under the first sun to enter the valley. And, above this, at the tree-line, children can be heard shouting across the slopes as they collect forage for the animals. The path narrows and slowly the slopes close out Taganana. The only noticeable landmark will be a sprawling mass of large grey lichen-covered boulders running down the slope on your left.

At **2h**, from a pass, you overlook two very different valleys: the Taganana is a large valley, with sharp outlines and enormous salients of rock jutting out of the landscape, while the Afur valley is a mould of ridges

The scattered houses of Afur and the surrounding razor-edged ravines characteristic of the Anaga range (Picnic 21; Walks 21 and 23; near Car tours 2 and 4).

and gulleys. Lone dwellings perch on these ridges, above the valleys that slice up the landscape. Roque de Dentro rises out of the sea far in the background, over on the Taganana side of the ridge. *The Short walk turns back here.*

To head on to Afur, keep right and downhill on an earthen path. Ignore a track turning off to the right two minutes down. Ignore, too, all further forks. Sheltered by inconsistent patches of tree heather, this path takes you down to the first habitations, 20 minutes downhill from the crest. Here you join a track/concrete drive; ignore a fork off to the right a minute downhill. Just around the bend is a cheerful house: its façade tries to match the colours in its garden. The track drops steeply. In a further 15 minutes it joins the road leading to Afur, where you bear right downhill, accompanied by the sounds of a babbling brook. Some 20 minutes down the road, below a small parking bay on the left, descend steps into the village nucleus (**2h55min**). The centre is just a church, a bar/shop, and a few modest houses.

Your continuation to Taborno is not signposted. It starts just behind the tall electricity substation that you passed on your way down into Afur, just before the church. Follow this path down to a confluence of streams, an ideal picnic spot. There are few places on Tenerife where the water flows so abundantly, and even this source dries to a trickle in high summer. A small concrete bridge takes you over the first stream, from where you make your way through boulders to the second stream crossing a minute later. Cascading water fills an already-overflowing pool.

Once over the second bridge, head up the ridge; don't bear right. *Asphodelus,* with its long, thin, blade-like leaves and white flowering stalks, covers the slope, along with scatterings of purple *Senecio.* The view back to Afur from here shows its superb setting, as the great wall of rock plays guardian to the little houses in its niches. When the path next forks, either route will take you to your next landfall, another small settlement. Your way veers left and heads down

Taganana (Picnic 23, Car tour 2)

past the houses. Rock walls, a deep mauve in colour, and untamed clumps of prickly-pear cactus prevent you from catching more than a fleeting glimpse of the individual houses. Ten minutes further up, come upon a lone house. At a fork a few minutes beyond it, go right. Then keep right all the way up.

You will be surprised to find yet another group of houses. Concealed from the rest of the valley, they are set back safely into the side of the ridge. Dogs barking will bring out children, and you will be welcomed with waves and giggles. Your path turns off to the right of the houses. From above them, you have a superb outlook: the view catches all the small dwellings sheltering behind rocky ridges and in corners of the valley. Roque Negro, a solid mass of black rock rising up from the slopes and encircled by trees at its base, stands out well, slightly to your right. A few minutes later, by a water tap on the crest, you can enjoy views down to the beach. This is the local laundry spot, but the water is also drinkable. The two farmhouses, a little below you to the left, are the last of the solitary homes before Taborno. Make for the track above the houses and follow it to the right. Taborno (photograph page 102) soon comes into view, and the first dwellings greet you at under **4h**. Red-flowering aloes cheer your approach to the large, open square, from where there are tremendous views across the razor-sharp ridges.

Las Carboneras is now just over on the next ridge. To reach the path, follow the tarred road out of Taborno for about 10 minutes. No sign marks your turn-off, but a keen eye will spot the path on the right. You reach it through a gap in the roadside barrier. Your only landmark is a fairly large rock sitting just off the road, to the right of the path. The crest of a steep ridge now becomes your way. The remains of an old shrine, embedded in the slope a few minutes downhill on your left, will assure you it's the correct route. Just down from the shrine, the path forks. Keep left and head towards the green plots. The bottom of the *barranco* is where you are heading, so don't take any turn-offs.

At about **4h25min** you cross a stream running down the *barranco*. From here on, it's a steady climb. Cross another trickle of water (in winter only) and keep right beyond it. Plots and grassy slopes lead you to a tarred road. The bus stop is on your right, exactly where you enter Las Carboneras (**5h10min**).

24 EL BAILADERO • CHINOBRE • CABEZO DEL TEJO • EL DRAGUILLO • ALMACIGA

Map on reverse of the fold-out touring map; see also photographs pages 18, 30-31

Distance: 10km/6.2mi; 6h

Grade: moderate-strenuous; ascent of 300m/1000ft, followed by a steep descent of 800m/2600ft

Equipment: walking boots, cardigans, anorak, raingear, whistle, picnic, water

How to get there: 🚌 102 from Puerto to Santa Cruz (Timetable 1); journey time 1h; *change to* 🚌 246 (Timetable 14); journey time 35min. Leave the bus at the El Bailadero stop (this is before the tunnel, under the viewpoint).
To return: 🚌 246 from Almáciga to Santa Cruz (Timetable 14); journey time 55min; *change to* 🚌 102 to Puerto (as above)

Alternative walk: Almáciga — El Draguillo — Almáciga: 9km/5.6mi; 3h45min; moderate climb/descent of 300m/1000ft; equipment as above. Take 🚌 246 bus from Santa Cruz to Almáciga and back (Timetable 14); journey time 55min. Use the map on the reverse of the touring map to reach El Draguillo by track; return the same way.

Your journey begins along the coast, as you leave Santa Cruz, and it finishes high above the coast as you walk to Almáciga. In between, high forested mountain trails rise and fall over moss-cushioned crests. Remains of the original laurel forests darken and roof your way. Unsurpassed views lie at regular intervals along this spine of the Anaga range.

Your bus stop is just before a road tunnel that takes the TF1124 into the Taganana Valley. Although you've bought a ticket for El Bailadero, reaching this *mirador* involves a 15-minute hike. **The path begins** just across the road from the parking area/bus stop. Keep right at the junction under 10 minutes up. Come to the TF1123 and bear right (a bar/restaurant is to your left). Follow this road for the next half hour. At about **45min**, at a sign for 'El Pijara', climb a path on your left. Through the trees you can see your destination, Almáciga, far below. Bear left at a fork some 10 minutes up the path. Beyond here, keep to the main path, ignoring all turn-offs downhill to the left.

Canary bellflower (Campanula canariensis)

When you leave the trees and meet the road, head down it to the left. Within 10 minutes you come to the Anaga Forestry Park (**2h**; Picnic 24a), an ideal, shady picnic spot with many tables and benches on both sides of the road. From here climb a track on your left, signposted 'Cabezo del Tejo' and

In the laurel forest, between Chinobre and Roque Anambro (Walks 24 and 25)

Chinobre' (don't follow the track on your *far* left). Soon the track narrows to a path. About 35 minutes up, turn left to the Chinobre Mirador, a rocky nodule at 909m/2980ft (**2h35min**; Picnic 24b). This is one of the best viewing points on the whole island, equalled only by Teide and Guajara. Your views encompass El Teide, Santa Cruz, San Andrés, Taganana, Taborno and Almáciga. Multitudes of ridges dissect the backbone of the Anaga into narrow, isolated valleys.

Back on the main path, turn left. A minute downhill, again fork left. You're now walking in the setting shown above. At about **3h15min** you come face-to-face with a large projection of rock towering above the trees. This bare-faced rock is called Anambro, and it provides another good viewpoint over the hidden northern valleys. Cabezo del Tejo (**3h45min**) is yet another magnificent look-out, with panoramas to the west.

At the end of this viewpoint, a sign for El Draguillo marks your steeply-descending path. On coming to a junction, turn left. Once you emerge from the trees, El Draguillo discloses itself sitting back on the sea-cliffs. From these heights, the village is a tight bunch of dulled rooftops, smothered in prickly pear (photograph pages 30-31). At just over **4h30min** you meet the 'King of Dragons', outside the village. It is, of course, for this dragon tree that the village was named. But 'El Draguillo' means the *little* dragon tree, and it certainly has grown in the intervening years!

Below the tree, ignore the track off right (to Las Palmas). Bear left on a gravel road, accompanied by stunning coastal scenery. At Benijo (Picnic 24c) the way becomes tarred, and you remain on the road to the Almáciga turn-off. The village crowns a hilltop (photograph page 18), ten minutes up from the TF1124 (**6h**). The bus stops at the shelter near the church.

25 EL BAILADERO • CHINOBRE • BARRANCO DE UJANA • LAS CASILLAS • IGUESTE

Map on reverse of touring map; see also photograph page 117

Distance: 11km/6.8mi; 5h45min

Grade: moderate-strenuous, with an ascent of 300m/1000ft and a slippery descent of 900m/3000ft on overgrown paths. *Recommended for experienced and adventurous walkers only.*

Equipment: walking boots, cardigans, anorak, raingear, long trousers long-sleeved shirt, picnic, water

How to get there: 🚌 102 from Puerto to Santa Cruz (Timetable 1) journey time 1h; *change to* 🚌 246 (Timetable 14); journey time 35min. Leave the bus at the El Bailadero stop (this is before the tunnel, under the viewpoint).

To return: 🚌 245 from Igueste to Santa Cruz (Timetable 15); journey time 30min; *change to* 🚌 102 to Puerto (as above)

Shorter walk: El Bailadero — Chinobre — El Bailadero: 8.5km/5.3mi 3h55min; fairly strenuous ascent/descent of 300m/1000ft; equipment as above. Follow the main walk for 2h35min and return the same way. Access as above and the same buses to return.

This walk takes you from the heights of the Anaga down to the quiet coastal village of Igueste. Your trail is down the dark, damp interior of Barranco de Ujana, full of the exuberant, jungle-like vegetation which makes up the laurel forest. Only flickers of light

On the approach to Las Casillas (Picnic 25a)

manage to penetrate this dense covering of forest. Ferns block your path, tired old trees are mummified in thick green moss, and the canary — no longer a common sight — adds a note of cheer with its chirpy whistle. Las Casillas, a hamlet long abandoned, makes a perfect lunch stop, nestled high on a rocky crest. Igueste, where the trek ends, is a delightful village, where trees and neatly-tended plots overflow the sides of the valley.

Start out by following Walk 24 (page 116), to Chinobre (**2h35min**). From this marvellous look-out point, return to the main path and keep left. A minute downhill, again fork left. This path, also followed in Walk 24 (photograph page 117), leads towards Cabezo del Tejo, but you will leave it in 10 minutes. Your turn-off, on the right, is obscure, but has definite waymarkers: it comes up just after you have descended some earthen steps, and there is a *sendero turístico* sign nailed high on a tree, a metre/yard *beyond* your turn-off.

Turn right down the V in the slope: there is *no* real path. In five minutes, when you reach an earthen track, bear right. Three minutes (130m/yds) along this track, look out for a *sendero turístico* sign on your right, on the embankment (about 3m/10ft above the track). Just 35m/yds beyond this sign find your downhill 'path' again, on a bend. You head back into the forest (**2h 55min**), following a narrow streambed down the *barranco*. You may have to negotiate a fallen tree, but a path becomes obvious in a minute: veer right on it, out of the streambed. Continue through undergrowth and over fallen trees, until you reach another track (**3h 05min**). Here, on your left, you'll see a sign, 'Hoya Ujana'. Bear left downhill on the track for a few metres/yards, until you can bear right on your densely-matted path. There are *no* waymarks here. Once again, you're in a streambed. A few minutes down, the gulley is too muddy and slippery to continue: cross to the left-hand side of the stream and follow the small path downhill for one minute, then make your way back down to the streambed (probably on your backside), *before it turns sharply to the right.* Now cross the streambed and make your way up the right-hand side of the ravine, always keeping the stream within sight. Your route becomes an obstacle course, as you climb over fallen trees and push your way through bushes.

Under 10 minutes after crossing the streambed you begin a series of stream crossings at one- or two-minute intervals. It's near this permanent water source that you'll hear (and with any luck, see) canaries. Keep alert. The last crossing brings you to a tiny dam (the second one) in the stream. Across the stream, there are two large water tanks (**3h35min**). Pick up the continuation of your path beyond and below these tanks (Picnic 25b). Don't cross the streambed; be sure to keep to the left of it.

At **3h40min** the TF1123 becomes your way: turn left downhill. In a few minutes, on a sharp bend, turn right down a clear loose-gravel path which takes you down through trees and past a cascade five minutes later. Yams grow alongside the streambed. Ignore any small turn-offs to plots but, some 25 minutes downhill, bear left at a fork in the path. You now gradually leave the *barranco* behind as you begin ascending towards the crest of a ridge. Two minutes later, a path branches off right; keep left. Ignore paths ascending to the right, as well as a path to the left. The abandoned stone houses of Las Casillas (**4h20min**; Picnic 25a; photograph page 118) are built around, over and into this rocky crest.

From Las Casillas descend towards the Barranco de Igueste on the right, below the abandoned hamlet. You cross a ridge and continue down the right-hand side of it. Igueste awaits you far below. Some 15 minutes from Las Casillas, you are back on the ridge again. Just over a minute later, you come to the Igueste turn-off: 30m/yds beyond the last pole on the top of the ridge, head down to the right through large arms of *cardón*. No turn-offs are necessary. At **5h20min** tar comes underfoot. Meet the main road and head left to the bus terminus/car park on the east side of the *barranco* (**5h45min**).

The beach at Igueste (Walks 25 and 27; Picnic 27; Car tour 2)

26 CHAMORGA • ROQUE BERMEJO • FARO DE ANAGA • TAFADA • CHAMORGA

Map on reverse of touring map; see photographs pages 18, 30-31
Distance: 7km/4.3mi; 4h05min

Grade: strenuous descent/ascent of 600m/1950ft; **danger of vertigo.** Those who suffer badly from vertigo will find the return path *impassable;* this can be avoided by returning along the outgoing path.

Equipment: stout shoes (boots preferable), cardigans, anorak, raingear, picnic, water, whistle

How to get there and return: hired car or taxi to Chamorga

Alternative walk: Chamorga — Roque Bermejo — Faro de Anaga — El Draguillo — Almáciga: 13km/8mi; 6h30min; strenuous (overall ascent 400m/1300ft; overall descent 950m/3100ft); equipment and access as above. This walk, somewhat easier than the main hike, visits some of the most spectacular scenery on Tenerife. Follow the main walk to the 2h10min-mark, where it leaves the main path to head up a crest to Tafada. Instead, keep straight along the main path. Ten minutes from the turn-off, come to a pleasant picnic spot, by a spring. Meet a first junction, just past an enormous boulder: head right, then bear left *immediately*. A few minutes later, bear left again. You come into Las Palmas at about 3h. Now either follow the sea cliffs (always keeping right) or, if you suffer from vertigo, go *left* at the junction and up through Las Palmas: head up past the three houses and turn left after the third one. A minute or two later (5min from the junction), turn right and pass an old chapel. In a few minutes you rejoin the sea-cliff path, reaching El Draguillo (photograph pages 30-31) at about 4h, half a minute down from a junction. From here take the track to Almáciga (photograph page 18), 2h30min away.

Chamorga, a serene little village, beautifully sited in the isolated north-eastern tip of the island, is where your hike begins and ends. From Chamorga you follow a narrow, shaded ravine that winds its way down to the idyllic bay of Roque Bermejo, only accessible on foot or by boat. An old lighthouse, still manned, gives warning of Roque Bermejo — a sharp, reddish peak clinging onto the edge of the island far below. Rocky crests, with clear sea views down grassy slopes, return you to Chamorga. Closer to the village, you may see evidence of the old method of charcoal making, whereby wood is left to smoulder under a pile of damp earth. Though very much outdated, this is still done in the poorer, more remote areas of Tenerife.

Begin the walk in the village square. Head down into the ravine on the path at the left-hand side of the chapel. Half a minute down, a sign for 'Roque Bermejo' points you to the right. Cane fills the moist valley floor. Five minutes downhill, a water tap offers you your last chance of a drink. This path takes you to the beach, without any turn-offs, so put your book away and amble on. A small stream idles its way down the ravine, replenishing stagnant pools. A view of a white house, set in the V of the *barranco,* will be your first landmark as the ravine opens out to the nearby sea (**40min**). Now a wide path suggests civilisation, as it makes its way up from the sea. A minute later, a large rock sitting off the tip of the island comes into view — Roque Bermejo.

The lighthouse solves the mystery of the wide path, as you round the ridge five minutes later. At **45min** you reach a couple of old houses, joined together, overlooking a small basin. Below, in the ravine, are overflowing tanks of water in store for the long dry summer and curtailing any would-be cascades. The basin, hemmed in by high escarpment walls, is a wealth of produce. A solitary family living here is responsible for all this work. To get down to these plots, turn left at the old building and make your way down the steep path. Take a deep breath and enjoy the scent from the Canarian lavender bushes. You pass by a small cottage, well-concealed behind shrubs and trees, in the centre of this cultivation.

Signs at an intersection (**55min**), point out all your directions: 'El Faro' and 'Las Palmas' to the left, 'Bermejo' to the right. Turn right. A few minutes downhill, you come to a small chapel and a large deserted house, from where there is a tremendous view down into the bay. A sign indicates that this is the settlement of Roque Bermejo. In under 10 minutes you'll reach the port area and the stony beach. A few fishermen's cottages lie over to the right. At the foot of Roque Bermejo sits a well-protected, crystal-clear pool set in the rocks. However, this is only accessible at low tide. The port area offers good swimming, however, for confident swimmers. This beautiful enclosed rocky bay is encircled by the sheer slopes that mark the end of the island.

Back at the junction (**1h15min**), head straight up the wide old lighthouse path. The lighthouse (Faro de Anaga), some 50 minutes up, is a good place to recuperate from the steep climb (there's more to come) and to appreciate your surroundings. The continuation of your path clambers over rock, to the left of the lighthouse. On the crest of the ridge, behind the lighthouse, the Roques de Anaga are visible.

At about **2h10min** (five minutes up from the lighthouse and a minute or two up the crest), leave the main path and continue up a smaller one on your left, making for the crest above. This path heads straight up the ridge, so you can't go wrong. A black electricity cable to the lighthouse runs down the ridge (if you need reassurance). *The main path continues to Las Palmas and is the route of the Alternative walk.* Your route is up the very steep grassy slope; it affords good views over both sides of the lateral ridge as you ascend.

Eventually you leave the crest of the ridge and start moving inland, constantly climbing. As you rapidly gain height, the terrain becomes rockier and more sheer, with the possibility of vertigo for those unaccustomed to heights. Enormous *Aeoniums* plaster the bare rock faces. Pass through a metal and wooden gate and, some 10 minutes later, *beware:* the path *appears* to continue around the side of the slope, along the same contour. Your way, however, actually heads uphill to the *left,* over the rock surface. It is therefore hard to find. If you end up on an outcrop in the rocky slope, you know you've gone too far. Retrace your steps a few metres/yards and head up above it. Tafada, just a solitary stone farm building cradled in a dip in the ridge, makes a good viewing point at **3h20min**. From here you look straight down into the Barranco de Roque Bermejo.

To make for Chamorga, continue up the left-hand side of the ridge; a *very* narrow path will quickly show itself. Those who suffer from vertigo will find this path unnerving for a couple of minutes. As you round a crest three minutes later, the school — slightly apart from the rest of the village — comes into sight in the distance. At this point, the path begins descending. A steep rock face embedded in the slope slows you up a bit, as you scale down it using both hands and feet. This is another place where *those prone to vertigo may well find themselves unable to continue.* It's here that you may see the charcoal burners — great puffs of smoke reveal their location.

Chamorga appears at **3h50min**. From this viewpoint, it's picture postcard-perfect (Picnic 26). As you descend, notice the rock at the end of this crest: it resembles a dog's head. Cumbrilla sits safely across the valley on a parallel ridge. Some 15 minutes down, you reach the first houses and a bar/shop (**4h05min**). Take some refreshment on board before returning to your transport; in particular, be sure to sample the superb local wine and goats' cheese.

27 IGUESTE • MONTAÑA DE ATALAYA • BARRANCO DE ZAPATA • PLAYA DE ANTEQUERA • IGUESTE

Map on reverse of touring map; photographs page 120

Distance: 9km/5.6mi; 5h30min

Grade: very strenuous, with total ascents/descents of over 900m/3000ft; **danger of vertigo.** *Recommended for expert walkers only.*

Equipment: walking boots, cardigans, anorak, sunhat, raingear, whistle, picnic, water

How to get there: 🚌 102 from Puerto to Santa Cruz (Timetable 1); journey time 1h; *change to* 🚌 245 to Igueste (Timetable 15); journey time 30min

To return: buses as above

Short walk: Igueste — 'Semáforo' — Igueste: 6km/3.7mi; 3h10min; strenuous ascent/descent of 400m/1300ft, but no danger of vertigo. Equipment and access as main walk. Follow the main walk for 1h40min, then continue to the Semáforo, the old abandoned lighthouse. Return the same way.

Playa de Antequera lies in one of the most beautiful bays on Tenerife. The fact that it is only accessible by boat or on foot makes this tranquil little harbour even more special. From the heights of Montaña de Atalaya, this hidden cove is truly magnificent, the sun reflecting off its blue waters. A high arm of rock — the Roque de Antequera — extending out into the sea, protects it from the northeasterly winds. The friendly Antequera beach caretaker, his wife and dog are the only signs of life you'll encounter.

A short coastal ride above small, sandy coves set in the cliffs brings you to Igueste (de San Andrés), your starting point. This proud little village, with its well-tended groves of mangoes, avocados, guavas and bananas, sits just up from the sea, inside the Barranco de Igueste. Stay on the bus to the end of the route (a turning point and bus shelter on the *east* bank of the stream).

Start out by following a paved path ('Casas de Abajo'), then turn left into Pasate Julio, heading towards a red/white TV aerial. Turn left at the aerial (white dot) towards the cemetery. At the top of a flight of steps there is a white arrow indicating your path (on the left) and a white waymark on the rock. The start of this earthen path is rather insignificant, but it widens out and becomes obvious within a few metres/yards.

You leave the village behind in **20min**, heading for an old lighthouse. This tower ('Semáforo') was used before the days of radio, to send hand-signals. Chiselled out of the slope, your path climbs relentlessly. *Euphor-*

bia, various cacti and bright green, drooping *valo,* with its soft, needle-like leaves, cover the hillside. White chrysanthemums are in full bloom in spring. A prominent rock, standing upright just off the path, makes a good viewpoint (in about **1h**) over the coastline towards Santa Cruz.

Aeonium nobile

Just before the path evens out (**1h40min**), you must turn turn left and clamber over a rough, rocky trail to the crest of this ridge. (A section of rock wall which you will have just begun following has crumbled away just where you branch off left.) *The Short walk continues from here to the lighthouse.* When you reach the crest, continue to your left; five minutes should bring you to a derelict old chapel (**1h50min**). Igueste lies far below, set above the groves of fruit trees. Montaña de Atalaya, on your right just a few minutes away (marked by a conspicuous white pillar), is the best spot for viewing Playa de Antequera. There's no path to the summit, but it's a very straightforward climb. Beyond here the way is fairly well waymarked either with dots of green paint or white arrows, and the usual small cairns. Sometimes an X indicates 'wrong way'.

Ranunculus cortusifolius

Red-flowering tabaiba (Euphorbia atropurpurea)

Beyond the chapel you will have to *watch carefully* for your turn-off into the Barranco de Zapata, the stream leading towards Antequera: from the crest, descend for about 15 minutes, to a point where the path has levelled out, then bear right on the narrow path. The way is difficult to follow for the next 20 minutes or so, continually fading. Sometimes the way splits into as many as three

Vinagrera (Rumex lunaria)

Senecio

Codéso (Adenocarpus foliolosus)

Margarita (Argyranthemum)

Valo (Plocama pendula)

Retama

different paths, but they all rejoin sooner or later and reach the beach. The idea is to head straight for the bottom of the *barranco.* Descending rapidly, you drop through the remains of old terraced plots into the valley below. Before reaching the bottom, you cross over a dry streambed on your right (about 20 minutes down). A concealed, overgrown clump of fig trees, in a narrow side-gorge, reveals itself as you pass through it some three minutes further along.

You reach the *barranco* floor in about **2h10min** and cross a dry streambed above a dry cascade. From here on, remain on the left side of the Barranco de Zapata, as you gradually ascend. Dark, gaping holes mark the hillsides. *Cardón* adds a touch of severity to the slopes. Another dry streambed is crossed before the way climbs again. Ignore paths heading streamward. Shepherds, making use of a sheltered rocky overhang, have built a couple of small pens about four minutes further on. Five minutes past the pens you must clamber straight up for a couple of metres/yards (just beyond a dry watercourse). Then head right, along the steep rock face; in a minute or two, you will find the path again.

A dyke, obliterating the bay as it slices its way seaward down the escarpment, stops you in your tracks at about **2h30min**, and a small rock arch frames the serene beauty of the Playa de Antequera. You pass through the arch and then bear left immediately, to head uphill. Vertigo is a definite possibility here — the path clings to this very steep, sheer slope. High above the sea, this goats' path is very narrow and involves clambering over large patches of rocky surface. *Tabaiba* and more brilliant green *valo* bushes cover the slopes.

Just before rounding a ridge, the path continues down to the right, above another *barranco.* Here, just on the nose of the ridge, you leave the path and scramble down to your right to the sandy (if it's low tide) Playa de Antequera below (**3h**). Two lone dwellings, one the caretaker's residence, sit in a gentle curve in the slopes above the beach, and a small harbour with an abandoned bar lies at the end of it.

When you've decided to head back, clamber up the steep sandy bank, until you come to a path, about 10-15 minutes uphill. Your landmarks on the return will be: the dyke, the old pens, and the crossing to the other side of the *barranco.* This section, up to the path leading to the derelict old chapel, is slightly more difficult in this direction, as the way keeps fading from view. Once you've crossed the dry streambed beyond the fig trees, head more or less straight up and you'll soon meet the path. The next spot of difficulty lies after the old chapel: five minutes beyond it, you leave the crest of the ridge. A flat, circular piece of rock, just on the crest, marks the turn-off. Here, your path returns to the Semáforo path and then leads down to Igueste, which you reach about 2h30min from the Playa de Antequera (**5h30min**). The rocky beach here at Igueste (see page 120) is a lovely place to while away the time before your bus departs.

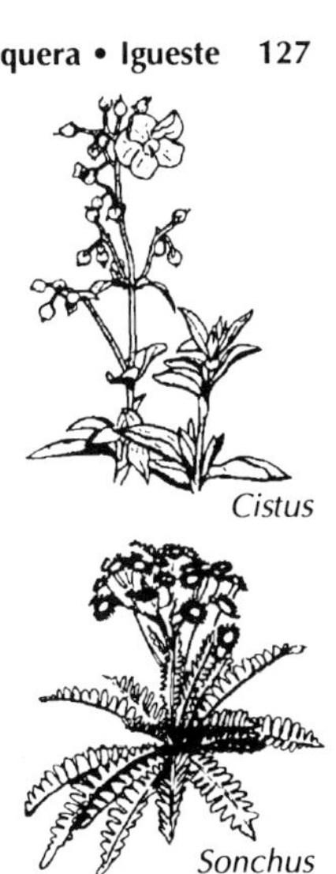

Cistus

Sonchus ortunoi

Palo sangre (Sonchus tectifolius)

Sea lavender (Crithmum maritimum)

Andryala cheiranthifolia

BUS TIMETABLES

Below is a list of destinations covered by the following pages of timetables, which give access to all the walks in the book. Numbers following place names are **timetable numbers**. There are more buses *and departures* than those listed here; see latest TITSA timetables.

Afur 17
Aguamansa 2, 5
Almáciga 14
Arona 9
Bailadero, El 14
Benijos 10
Buenavista 6, 11
Caldera, La 2
Cañadas, Las Parador, Visitors' Centre 5, 9
Carboneras, Las 16
Casa Negrín 16, 17
Cruz de Taganana 17, 18
Cruz del Carmen 16, 18
Erjos 7
Guancha, La 4
Icod de los Vinos 4, 6, 7, 8
Icod el Alto 4
Igueste 15
Laguna, La 1, 13, 16-19
Llanos, Los 7
Montaña Blanca 5, 9
Montañeta, La
above Icod 8
near El Palmar 11
Orotava, La 2, 3, 5, 10
Palmar, El 11
Palo Blanco 10
Pico del Inglés 16-19
Playa de las Américas 9, 12
Portelas, Las 11
Portillo, El 5, 9
Puerto de la Cruz 1-6
Punta del Hidalgo 13
Realejo Alto 10
Roque Negro 17, 18
Santa Cruz 1, 12-15
Taborno 16
Taganana 14
Teide funicular 5, 9
Vega, La 8
Vilaflor 9

1 102: Puerto de la Cruz to Santa Cruz; EXPRESS; daily

Puerto	La Laguna	Santa Cruz
07.15	08.00	08.15
	then every 30 minutes until	
21.15	22.00	22.15

Santa Cruz	La Laguna	Puerto
07.30	07.45	08.30
	then every 30 minutes until	
20.30	20.45	21.30
21.15	21.30	22.15

2 345: Puerto de la Cruz to La Caldera; daily

Puerto	La Orotava	Aguamansa	La Caldera
07.00*	07.15*	08.00*	—
08.00*	08.15*	09.00*	—
08.45	09.00	09.45	09.50
	and every 45 minutes until		
17.15	17.30	18.15	18.20

La Caldera	Aguamansa	La Orotava	Puerto
10.00	10.05	10.50	11.05
	and every 45 minutes until		
18.25	18.30	19.15	19.30
—	19.15*	20.00*	20.15*
—	20.00*	20.45*	21.00*
—	20.45*#	21.30*#	—
—	21.15*	22.00*	22.15*

*terminates/starts out from Aguamansa; #only to La Orotava

3 350: Puerto de la Cruz to La Orotava; daily

Puerto	La Orotava
06.30	06.45
and every 30 minutes until	
23.00	23.15

La Orotava	Puerto
06.30	06.45
and every 30 minutes until	
23.30	23.45

4 354: Puerto de la Cruz to Icod de los Vinos; daily

Puerto	Icod el Alto	La Guancha	Icod de los Vinos
07.30	08.05	08.15	08.30
	and every hour on the half hour until		
20.30	21.05	21.15	21.30

Icod de los Vinos	La Guancha	Icod el Alto	Puerto
08.00	08.15	08.45	09.00
	and every hour on the half hour until		
20.00	20.15	20.45	21.00

5 348: Puerto de la Cruz to Las Cañadas; daily

Puerto (depart)	09.15	**Parador** (depart)	16.00
La Orotava	09.30	**Teide funicular**	16.15
Aguamansa	10.15	**Montaña Blanca**	16.30
El Portillo	10.45	**Visitors' Centre**	16.40
Visitors' Centre	10.50	**El Portillo**	16.45
Montaña Blanca	11.00	**Aguamansa**	17.15
Teide funicular	11.15	**La Orotava**	18.00
Parador	11.30	**Puerto**	18.15

6 363: Puerto de la Cruz to Buenavista; daily

Puerto	San Juán	Icod de los Vinos	Buenavista
06.00	06.20	06.45	07.45
	and every hour on the hour until		
22.00	22.20	22.45	23.45
Buenavista	**Icod de los Vinos**	**San Juán**	**Puerto**
06.30	07.30	07.55	08.15
	and every hour on the hour until		
20.30*	21.30*	—	—

*the bus at 20.30 terminates at Icod de los Vinos; all others go through to Puerto

7 460: Icod de los Vinos to Guía de Isora; daily

Icod	Erjos	Los Llanos turn-off	Santiago	Guía de Isora
07.30	08.05	08.10	08.15	08.45
10.00	10.35	10.40	10.45	11.15
12.00	12.35	12.40	12.45	13.15
14.15	14.50	14.55	15.00	15.30
16.00	16.35	16.40	16.45	17.15
18.00	18.35	18.40	18.45	19.15
20.15	20.50	20.55	21.00	21.30
Guía de Isora	**Santiago**	**Los Llanos turn-off**	**Erjos**	**Icod**
07.45	08.15	08.20	08.25	09.00
10.00	10.30	10.35	10.40	11.15
11.45	12.15	12.20	12.25	13.00
14.15	14.45	14.50	14.55	15.30
16.00	16.30	16.35	16.40	17.15
18.00	18.30	18.35	18.40	19.15
19.45	20.15	20.20	20.25	21.00

8 360: Icod de los Vinos to La Montañeta (San José bus); daily

Icod	La Montañeta	*La Vega*	La Montañeta	Icod
07.15	07.50	*lies half-*	12.15	12.50
11.30	12.05	*way between*	16.00	16.35
15.15	15.50	*Icod and*	19.15	19.50
18.30	19.05	*La Montañeta*	20.40	21.15

9 342: Playa de las Américas to Las Cañadas; daily

Playa de las Américas (depart)	09.15	**El Portillo** (depart)	15.15
Los Cristianos	09.30	**Visitors' Centre**	15.20
Arona	09.40	**Montaña Blanca**	15.30
Vilaflor	10.00	**Teide funicular**	15.40
Parador	11.00	**Parador**	16.00
Teide funicular	11.15	**Vilaflor**	17.00
Montaña Blanca	11.30	**Arona**	17.20
Visitors' Centre	11.40	**Los Cristianos**	17.30
El Portillo	11.45	**Playa de las Américas**	17.45

10 347: La Orotava to Realejo Alto; daily

La Orotava	Benijos	Palo Blanco	Cruz Santa	Realejo Alto
09.10	09.30	09.40	09.50	10.00
11.05	11.25	11.35	11.45	11.55
13.05	13.25	13.35	13.45	13.55
15.05	15.25	15.35	15.45	15.55
17.05	17.25	17.35	17.45	17.55
19.10	19.30	19.40	19.50	20.00
Realejo Alto	**Cruz Santa**	**Palo Blanco**	**Benijos**	**La Orotava**
10.05	10.15	10.25	10.35	10.55
12.05	12.15	12.25	12.35	12.55
14.05	14.15	14.25	14.35	14.55
16.05	16.15	16.25	16.35	16.55
18.05	18.15	18.25	18.35	18.55
20.05	20.15	20.25	20.35	20.55

11 366: Buenavista to Las Portelas; daily

Buenavista	El Palmar		El Palmar	Buenavista
		Mondays to Fridays		
07.30	07.45*		08.05#	08.20
09.30	09.45*		10.05#	10.20
13.15	13.30*		14.05#	14.20
17.30	17.45*		18.05#	18.20
19.30	19.45*		20.05#	20.20
		Sat, Sun/holidays		
07.30	07.45*		08.05#	08.20
11.30	11.45*		12.05#	12.20
13.30	13.45*		14.05#	14.20
15.15	15.30*		16.05#	16.20
19.30	19.45*		20.05#	20.20

*arrives La Montañeta and Las Portelas 5min later; #departs Las Portelas amd La Montañeta 5min earlier

12 111: Santa Cruz to Playa de las Américas; daily

Santa Cruz	La Candelaria	Poris de Abona	Los Cristianos	Playa Américas
		Mondays to Fridays		
06.00	06.15	06.50	07.25	07.30
		and every 40minutes until		
20.40	20.55	21.30	22.05	22.10
		Saturdays, Sundays and holidays		
06.30	06.45	07.20	07.55	08.00
		and every hour on the half hour until		
21.30	21.45	22.20	22.55	23.0
Playa Américas	**Los Cristianos**	**Poris de Abona**	**La Candelaria**	**Santa Cruz**
		Mondays to Fridays		
06.00	06.05	06.40	07.15	07.30
		and every 40minutes until		
21.20	21.25	22.00	22.35	22.50
		Saturdays, Sundays and holidays		
06.30	06.35	07.10	07.45	08.00
		and every hour on the half hour until		
21.30	21.35	22.10	22.45	23.00

13 105: Santa Cruz to Punta del Hidalgo; daily

Santa Cruz	La Laguna	Tegueste	Bajamar	Punta Hidalgo
07.35	08.05	08.20	08.30	08.45
		and every 30min until		
19.35	20.05	20.20	20.30	20.45
Punta Hidalgo	**Bajamar**	**Tegueste**	**La Laguna**	**Santa Cruz**
08.00	08.10	08.25	08.40	09.10
		and every 30min until		
20.00	20.10	20.25	20.40	21.10

14 246: Santa Cruz to Almáciga; daily

Santa Cruz	San Andrés	El Bailadero	Taganana	Almáciga
		Mondays to Fridays		
06.50	07.00	07.25	07.35	07.40
10.30	10.40	11.05	11.15	11.20
13.10	13.20	13.45	13.55	14.00
		Saturdays, Sundays and holidays		
07.05	07.15	07.40	07.50	07.55
09.10	09.20	09.45	09.55	10.00
11.30	11.40	12.05	12.15	12.20
14.10	14.20	14.45	14.55	15.00

Almáciga	Taganana	El Bailadero	San Andrés	Santa Cruz
		Mondays to Fridays		
14.10*	14.20*	14.30*	14.55*	—
15.45	15.55	16.05	16.30	16.40
18.00	18.10	18.20	18.45	18.55
20.05	20.15	20.25	20.50	21.00
		Saturdays, Sundays and holidays		
12.45	12.55	13.05	13.30	13.40
15.15	15.25	15.35	16.00	16.10
17.45	17.55	18.05	18.30	18.40
20.15	20.25	14.35	21.00	21.10

*only to San Andrés

15 245: Santa Cruz to Igueste; daily

Santa Cruz	Igueste		Igueste	Santa Cruz
		Mondays to Fridays		
07.25	07.55		12.30	13.00
09.10	09.40		15.10	15.40
11.50	12.20		17.10	17.40
14.25	14.55		19.10	19.40
16.10	16.40		21.10	21.40
08.40	09.10	*Sat, Sun/holidays*	13.30	14.00
10.30	11.00		15.30	16.00
12.30	13.00		19.30	20.00
14.30	15.00		21.30	22.00

Departures from San Andrés about 15min after Santa Cruz (outbound) or Igueste (inbound)

The following buses are currently operated by TRANSMERSA out of the main station near the motorway at La Laguna (see notes on page 7). If this changes in the future, the same station will be used.

16 1.705: La Laguna to Las Carboneras and Taborno; daily

La Laguna	Cruz del Carmen	Casa Negrín	Las Carboneras	Taborno
		Winter: Mondays to Fridays		
06.45	07.05	07.10	07.25	07.40
09.15	09.35	09.40	09.55	10.10
15.15	15.35	15.40	15.55	16.10

Taborno	Las Carboneras	Casa Negrín	Cruz del Carmen	La Laguna
16.30	16.15	16.45	16.50	17.10
19.30	19.15	19.45	19.50	20.10

Summer: Mondays to Fridays and year-round: Saturdays, Sundays and holidays

La Laguna	Cruz del Carmen	Casa Negrín	Las Carboneras	Taborno
07.30	07.50	07.55	08.10	08.25
15.00	15.20	15.25	15.40	15.55

Taborno	Las Carboneras	Casa Negrín	Cruz del Carmen	La Laguna
16.00	15.45	16.30	16.35	16.55
19.30*	19.15*	19.45*	19.50*	20.10*

*Not on Saturdays, Sundays or holidays

17 1.706: La Laguna to Afur and Roque Negro; daily**

Winter: Mondays to Fridays

La Laguna	Casa Negrín	Casa Forestal	Roque Negro	Afur
06.45	*not known*	07.35	07.50	08.00
13.15	*not known*	14.05	14.20	14.30
Afur	**Roque Negro**	**Casa Forestal***	**Casa Negrín**	**La Laguna**
14.45	14.55	15.10	*not known*	16.00
17.45	17.55	18.10	*not known*	19.00
20.00	20.10	20.25	*not known*	21.15

Summer: Mondays to Fridays

La Laguna	Casa Negrín	Casa Forestal	Roque Negro	Afur
06.55	*not known*	07.45	08.00	08.10
13.15	*not known*	14.05	14.20	14.30
Afur	**Roque Negro**	**Casa Forestal***	**Casa Negrín**	**La Laguna**
14.45	14.55	15.10	*not known*	16.00
17.45	17.55	18.10	*not known*	19.00
19.45	19.55	20.10	*not known*	21.00

Year-round: Saturdays, Sundays and holidays

La Laguna	Casa Negrín	Casa Forestal	Roque Negro	Afur
07.00	*not known*	07.50	08.05	08.15
13.15	*not known*	14.05	14.20	14.30
Afur	**Roque Negro**	**Casa Forestal***	**Casa Negrín**	**La Laguna**
14.45	14.55	15.10	*not known*	16.00
17.45	17.55	18.10	*not known*	19.00

*Also called 'Cruz de Taganana'; **bus should pass close to Casa Negrín, but *verify in advance!*

18 1.710: La Laguna to Casa Forestal*; *not daily*

Winter only: Mondays to Fridays

La Laguna	Cruz del Carmen	Pico del Inglés**	Roque Negro**	Casa Forestal
09.45	10.10	10.15	10.30	10.50
Casa Forestal	**Roque Negro****	**Pico del Inglés****	**Cruz del Carmen**	**La Laguna**
10.30	10.50	11.05	11.10	11.35

*Also called 'Cruz de Taganana'; **turn-off to

19 1.708: La Laguna to Pico del Inglés

Winter: Mondays to Fridays

La Laguna	Pico del Inglés*	Pico del Inglés*	La Laguna
10.15	10.45	10.45	11.15

Summer: Mondays to Fridays

La Laguna	Pico del Inglés*	Pico del Inglés*	La Laguna
09.15	09.45	09.45	10.15

Year-round: Saturdays

La Laguna	Pico del Inglés*	Pico del Inglés*	La Laguna
09.15	09.45	09.45	10.15

Year-round: Sundays and holidays

La Laguna	Pico del Inglés*	Pico del Inglés*	La Laguna
10.15	10.45	10.45	11.15

*turn-off to

Index

ieographical names comprise the only entries in this index. For all other entries, ɜe Contents, page 3. A page number in **bold type** indicates a photograph; a page umber in *italic type* indicates a map (both may be in addition to a text reference n the same page. 'TM' refers to the large-scale walking map of the Anaga eninsula on the reverse of the touring map. See also Timetable index, page 128. o save space, entries have been grouped under the following headings: Barranco iver or ravine), Choza (shelter), Faro (lighthouse), Galería (water gallery), Mirador 'iewpoint), Montaña (mountain), Playa (beach), Punta (point) and Zona recreativa icnic area with tables).